The Ascent to God

THE ASCENT TO GOD

Divine Theosis Revealed and Realized
in the Teaching of John Paul II

THOMAS P. KUFFEL
and NANCY CAROL JAMES

Foreword by Chad Zielinski

PICKWICK *Publications* · Eugene, Oregon

THE ASCENT TO GOD
Divine Theosis Revealed and Realized in the Teaching of John Paul II

Pickwick Publications
An Imprint of Wipf and Stock Publishers
199 W. 8th Ave., Suite 3
Eugene, OR 97401

www.wipfandstock.com

PAPERBACK ISBN: 978-1-7252-8548-4
HARDCOVER ISBN: 978-1-7252-8549-1
EBOOK ISBN: 978-1-7252-8550-7

Cataloguing-in-Publication data:

Names: Kuffel, Thomas P. [author]. | James, Nancy C., 1954- [author] | Zielinski, Chad [foreword writer]

Title: The ascent to God : divine theosis revealed and realized in the teaching of John Paul II / Thomas P. Kuffel and Nancy Carol James.

Description: Eugene, OR: Pickwick Publications, 2022 | Includes bibliographical references and index.

Identifiers: ISBN 978-1-7252-8548-4 (paperback) | ISBN 978-1-7252-8549-1 (hardcover) | ISBN 978-1-7252-8550-7 (ebook)

Subjects: LCSH: Deification (Christianity) | Mystical union | Beatific vision | John Paul II, Pope, 1920–2005 | Spirituality

Classification: BT767.8 K84 2022 (paperback) | BT767.8 (ebook)

VERSION NUMBER 030922

Nihil obstat: Reverend Marvin Samiano, JCL, Censor Liborum
Imprinatur: Most Reverend Larry Silva, Bishop of Honolulu. July 23, 2021.

We dedicate this book on St. John Paul's theosis to the holy nuns from Carmel of the Holy Trinity in Kailua, Hawaii, and their desire to encounter the living God abiding within their souls. May this work inspire them and all souls seeking the abiding presence of the Holy Trinity.

CONTENTS

FOREWORD

THE AMERICAN CATHOLIC AUTHOR Walker Percy correctly named our culture with the Greek term, the Thanatos Syndrome, the lover and follower of death instincts. A Thanatos culture sees problems, challenges, and suffering and proudly proclaims the answer lies in some form of death. A child is conceived with all his or her potentiality, both joys and challenges in the new life and the assumption of our current era says: solve this by killing the child. A person with a serious illness waits for the outcome of this and some say, Thanatos! Kill the patient now. With Physician Assisted Suicide, we even tell the doctor to kill the patient. With our changing values about the essence of human identity and dignity, we say Thanatos. Kill and end the debate and conversation allowed in previous centuries. This current philosophy promulgates that death conceived and completed by finite human beings solves everything. Yet looking at the results of these actions, we must ask ourselves: how do we find true life, abundant, overflowing, fulfilling?

St. John Paul II lived in an era where his governments had absolute power for the Thanatos Syndrome. Kill the Jews. Quiet the fervent Christians. End the practice of the Catholic faith. Brainwash the people to accept the truth of Thanatos, death of the human mind, soul, spirit, and body.

Yet our Catholic faith teaches the great truth of the Trinity that releases all humanity from the power of the Thanatos Syndrome. Every human being is made in the *imago dei*. As Augustine states, the sacred Trinity dwells within us, giving us life and the breath of the Holy Spirit.

St. John Paul II lived and preached this profound belief in the Trinity present in all human beings. After suffering under the Nazis and Communist regimes, he found a different way of living and spent his life proclaiming that we are to dwell in the Trinity and follow the Holy Spirit. Courageously, St. John Paul II, in the darkest time of Polish history, attended an underground seminary, while facing his own personal losses. Following the death of his mother, he lived sedately and quietly with his father, coming home one day to find the deceased body of his father. A brilliant man, St. John Paul II was forced to work in a factory, enduring the frustration of bodily fatigue while being denied the life of the Spirit and mind.

Thanatos, the love of death, surrounded him as his governments promulgated and forced this philosophy on unwilling people.

Yet St. John Paul II himself entirely rejected death, murder, revenge, hatred and all the accoutrements of death.

How did he do this? St. John Paul II lived a life dwelling in the actions of the Holy Spirit, becoming docile and submissive to the Spirit's motions. Because of this, his life became sure and certain. He led others to do the same. St. John Paul II, like all saints, was capable of unexpected and spiritual actions. He became the head of Oasis, a youth group in Poland, and invited an evangelist to preach in Europe. St. John Paul II supported Lech Walesa in his struggle for trade unions. He developed church movements, New Pentecost, and the New Evangelization, that emphasized the still-continuing actions of the Spirit.

St. John Paul II developed his theology continually. In his *Theology of the Body*, he described both the glories of married human sexuality and the glories of priestly celibacy. He threw open the doors of the Catholic Church to welcome suffering human beings and to let the heavenly light touch our profoundly wounded souls.

What do we call St. John Paul II's theology? The direct opposite of the Thanatos Syndrome. St. John Paul II affirms God's loving and passionate overtures to us, all of us, to let Jesus Christ into our hearts. As we do this, we grow in intimacy and union with the Trinity, Father, Son, and Holy Spirit. How should we spend our lives? Seeking the Face of God our Father.

When elected pope in an electrifying moment, St. John Paul II walked on the balcony telling us, "Do not be afraid!"

Why should we be courageous and faithful? In theological terms, we say Jesus Christ with Mary as co-mediatrix, crushed the skull of Lucifer, the Father of all lies and evil, a murderer from the beginning, the creator of Thanatos. We are not to fear because of this. In personal terms, we say St. John Paul II had lived his faith and experienced the efficacious actions of the Holy Spirit. We are not to fear because of this. In mystical terms, we say St. John Paul II lived his own spiritual development in *lectio divina* and theosis. The Second Vatican Council had given us the great gift of renewing our life in the Spirit based in the Word and the Father. We are not to fear because of this.

Now our own culture continues to grow in Thanatos, a death-loving culture. We humbly present St. John Paul II and his ideas of our participation in God, called theosis, to readers.

This is much needed at this time when our society is overwhelmed with confusion regarding the very nature of the human person. Fr. Tom Kuffel has dedicated much effort, time, and prayer to the accomplishment of this text. It is very well researched, reflecting the thought of St. John Paul II.

Fr. Kuffel's academic efforts are truly lived out in his daily ministry. At the local Church where he serves, Fr. Kuffel regularly engages with a group of individuals who struggle with addiction recovery, homelessness, domestic abuse, and violence. Like St. John Paul II, he passionately draws them into a conversation to help them see the Divine blueprint that lives within each person, radiating the beauty, goodness, and truth of our Creator.

I thank Fr. Kuffel and Dr. Nancy James for their dedication to have this work come to fruition. St. John Paul II's legacy intensely reflects the philosophy that each human person, imprinted with the life-giving presence of the Holy Trinity, possesses divine human dignity. Our prayers, our hope is that a ray of divine light from God's heart, mind, and soul enlightens our darkness, ending our own experience of Thanatos.

St. John Paul II leads us into new spiritual understanding of these most ancient of Christian practices, taught by the earliest Christian theologians and Church Fathers. May this book inspire our own perfection, our own docility to the Holy Spirit. May we ponder and embrace this theosis dwelling within each human soul from conception to natural death.

Bishop Chad Zielinski
Bishop of the Diocese of Fairbanks

PREFACE

THIS BOOK BEGAN IN a noon day mass in Fairbanks, Alaska, in the midnight sun, July 2019. Father Tom Kuffel, the pastor at Immaculate Conception Church, presided at the mass. The earliest church in Fairbanks, the beautiful white church was graced with a welcoming statue of Mary, clothed in blue with stars circling her head. The ICC organist, Nancy James, attended.

Father Tom preached on the scripture, "You therefore must be perfect as your heavenly Father is perfect." (Matt 5:48) Father Tom said, "Our Father gives us his perfection as a gift. God infuses this perfection within us, pouring his goodness, truth, and beauty within us."

A well-known Madame Guyon scholar, James sat astounded. Guyon called this divinization, while others called this theosis. This ancient belief in the Christian faith promised us participation in God and preparation for the Beatific Vision. Bernard of Clairvaux, John of the Cross, Madame Guyon, Archbishop Fénelon, and many other mystics described theosis. In recent centuries though, this crucial spiritual and mystical belief had quietly taken a back seat. With the spiritual awakening of the Second Vatican Council, St. John Paul II had written about this in his doctrine called the *Communio Personarum*.

After meeting, Kuffel and James began to write and received the blessing of Bishop Chad Zielinski to do so.

Theosis prepares us for the greatest of human blessings, the Beatific Vision of the Trinity, Father, Son, and Holy Spirit. Like the ten virgins waiting for the Divine Bridegroom, we fill our empty lamps with the oil of work and prayer, preparing for our divine participation and contemplation. This life-long journey of theosis allows the Holy Spirit to infuse us with the divine essence as expressed in the gifts of faith, hope, and love. Gifted with these theological virtues, theosis, divinization, the glories of the indwelling Trinity, awaits and welcomes us.

ACKNOWLEDGEMENTS

WE GRATEFULLY ACKNOWLEDGE THE great mystics, doctors, present, and past theologians within our Church's great tradition who inspired many of these ideas, concepts, and insights guiding us to the divine essence of the Beatific Vision. They challenge our devotions from being merely expressions of piety to become theological concepts rooted in a mature attitude that embraces the development not only of doctrine, but of our ability to delve deeply into the mysteries contained in Sacred Scripture. Through these studies, our minds experience the gifts of Understanding, Council, and Knowledge while our hearts embrace the Wisdom and Courage to live a life seeking the Beatific Vision.

We thank Melora Maria James for the photographs in this book.

We also personally thank those who have made contributions to our own understanding of theosis. Among many, we gratefully include the following: Jordan Aumann, OP, Fr. Andrew Byrne, Dr. Charles Price, and Dr. Carlos Eire.

IMAGES

INTRODUCTION

LONG FORGOTTEN IN THE annals of history, buried deep in the bowels of the papacy, this document "On the Beatific Vision of God" written by Pope Benedict XII reveals a doctrine essential to Christianity. This infallible statement defines the Beatific Vision, revealing the divine essence of the mystery of the Trinity. Pope Benedict XII writes that purified souls after death immediately see God face to face. In this most important papal encyclical, he writes the following:

> Since the passion and death of the Lord Jesus Christ, these souls have seen and see the divine essence with an intuitive vision and even face to face, without the mediation of any creature by way of object of vision; rather the divine essence immediately manifests itself to them, plainly, clearly and openly, and in this vision, they enjoy the divine essence.[1]

The beauty and wonder of this statement clarify the essence of the transcendent enjoyment of the Beatific Vision. Our fundamental vocation as a person created in the image and likeness of God lies in seeing through the veil this vision of the Father's Face

Created to abide with our Creator, we yearn for the power and presence of the Beatific Vision. We may behold this forgotten mystery that is slowly being exposed once again through the great renaissance of Sacred Scripture, the pinnacle fruit of the Second Vatican Council using the great angelic master, St. Thomas Aquinas. Through the writings of several popes and saints, including John Paul II, Paul VI, John XXIII, Benedict XVI and other great saints and mystics, we explore one of the greatest mysteries of the Catholic faith, the infusion of the Holy Spirit within us. St. John Paul called this the New Pentecost and the New Evangelization: united they

---

1. Benedict XII, *Benedictus Deus*, para. 1.

bring the missionary zeal to live, preach and teach this gift-love. In doing so, we realize our destiny to dwell within the Trinity, the *Divine Communio Personarum*. In theosis we seek and grow in perfection. This inborn principle of seeking the Divine Essence in the Beatific Vision guides our search for the Face of God the Father. Our search for theosis purifies us from the source of all Sin, the Fall, so that the recesses of the faithful heart are prepared for the reception of this Beatific Vision. To abide and behold the divine essence is to be truly blessed: perfected.

SEEKING THE BEATIFIC VISION

St. John Paul II dedicated this millennium of the twenty-first century to the contemplation of the Holy Face of God, infusing grace through the Holy Spirit in our souls longing for beauty. He writes the following.

> To contemplate the face of Christ, and to contemplate it with Mary, is the "programme" which I have set before the Church at the dawn of the third millennium, summoning her to put out into the deep on the sea of history with the enthusiasm of the new evangelization.[2]

St. John Paul II challenges us to seek the Holy Face of God and his idea of *Communio Personarum* shows us how to do this. Rooted in the Creation and Covenant, this signature doctrine opens to us the way to the Nuptial Banquet, revealing the Beatific Vision, the face of God the Father. St. John Paul's *Communio Personarum* encompasses his complete and total thought and in this we find the central motif of his powerful pontificate.

Communio creates the inspiration for his New Evangelization rooted in his experience of the New Pentecost. Pentecost constantly inspires. It inspires the desire that despite the Fall from Grace, we are perfectible and being perfectible we open ourselves to the subjectivity of the Divine. We are divine creations, and as divine images being perfected by the Holy Spirit, we cannot help but proclaim this Evangelium: Good News. I am perfectible by the power of the Spirit empowering me to live overshadowed by grace to bring the Good News of Christ to the whole world: He is present. He calls you his friend.

St. John Paul II's theology in "Letter to Artists" proclaims this powerful theology, calling us to participate and experience the Pathos of God

---

2. John Paul II, *Ecclesia de Eucharista*, sec. 6.

who created the universe with feeling and passion. Mystics experience and explore this original power in creation. Speaking directly to artists, St. John Paul II grounds contemplation profoundly in the scriptures and the mystical interpretations seen and revealed by the artists. Artists entering the most profound mystery unveil the *Communio Personarum*, "the image of an inscrutable divine communion of Persons."[3] This is the Beatific Vision.

The actions of God in creation once commenced never end. This continuance of the Divine Presence hovering constantly over creation grounds St. John Paul II's theology as he writes: "It is in the meeting between the Holy Spirit and the human spirit that we find the very heart of what the Apostles experienced at Pentecost. This extraordinary experience is present in the Church born of that event and accompanies her down the century. . . . Docility to the Spirit gives man continuous opportunities for life."[4]

Hence, God's act of creation in Genesis and the outpouring of the Spirit at Pentecost are continuing events that touch our mind, body, heart, and soul, causing theosis. St. John Paul II describes this as nourishment given to us for our interior life. He writes, "If evangelization requires holiness, in turn holiness requires the *nourishment of the spiritual life*: prayer and intimate union with God by means of the Word and of the Sacraments. In a word, it requires a profound and personal life of the Spirit."[5]

This contemplation of beauty of the Spirit calls to us. Pope Francis proclaims the impact of beauty in our faith.

> The perception and contemplation of beauty generates a sense of hope that can light up our world. The outer and inner movements merge and in turn affect our way of relating to those all around us. They generate empathy, the ability to understand others, with whom we have so much in common. We sense a bond with them, a bond no longer vague, but real and shared.[6]

So too St. John Paul II believes that beauty invites us to the *Divine Communio*, saying this transcendent reality calls us into goodness and truth and the indwelling of the Trinity. To participate in the Divine, we must experience the divine personally as it is an objective reality. It leads to a new consciousness of the awe and splendor of creation itself. In his doctoral dissertation, rather than defining speculative and theoretical

3. John Paul II, *Communion of Persons.*

4. John Paul II, *Solemnity of Pentecost*, sec. 3.

5. John Paul II, *Mass of Pentecost*, sec. 5.

6. Francis, "Artists of the Christmas Concert."

explanations, he maps out mystical experiences "without using technical terminology, but relying exclusively on experience and practice."[7] Through this mystical transformation—theosis—we experience God personally and participate in his Divine life.

Theosis or divinization then unites us with God experientially and this journey requires we live through the whole scriptural narrative from Genesis to Revelation using *lectio divina*. To complete the journey requires the application of Aquinas' four senses of scriptural interpretation. In these, St. Thomas unveils the divine participation of the soul in the Divine Essence. St. Thomas states that "in the nature of the soul does he participate in the Divine Nature, after the manner of a likeness, through a certain regeneration or re-creation."[8]

Our participation essentially communes with the Divine. We are made of the divine essence, not being deified as some pagan god, but adopted by the Father Who instills in us his essence. He forms us as *imago dei*, yet we cultivate this image by our free will. This insight, to choose to essentially participate in the *Communio Personarum*, is the ultimate pearl that we seek. In seeking, we awaken our memories and understanding of the original creation and covenant; experience the Fall; accept the plan for restoration; honor Mary as the Spouse of the Holy Spirit; recognize the power and mystery of the crucifixion and resurrection as our recreation; and discern our human destiny of the Beatific Vision lived in the New Jerusalem. In *lectio divina* and theosis, we participate in God's restoration of us into the *Divine Communio Personarum*, our coming perfection and glorification through theosis.

THE THREE STAGES OF THEOSIS

In the first stage, the Word of God instructs our mind, increasing our rational thinking ability and purifying our heart. We hunger for the transcendent insight of scripture and begin our ascent up Jacob's Ladder.

In the second stage, the Holy Spirit unites with the human will. This heart-felt connection with God creates a bond through which we are gradually led up the ladder. Our increasing submission to God's will creates a divine unity of purpose. The faithful look to Mary as the Spouse of the Holy Spirit who connects heaven and earth and show us the way to theosis.

7. John Paul II, *Faith*, 23.

8. Aquinas, *Summa Theologica*, I-II.110.4.

In the third stage, God chooses to sanctify the believer with an infusion of grace. This creates a purity of heart and will. Yet the believer must prepare through *Lectio Divina* for the reception and increase of this grace as it leads us directly to the Beatific Vision.

The yearning for theosis lies profoundly within our heart innately. God fully awakens in our heart the mysteries of the Incarnation of Christ: his life, crucifixion, resurrection, and ascension. We are completed by his Spirit descending upon us again at Pentecost recreating creation. Because of this, Thomas Aquinas' intuitive method of the interpretation of Sacred Scriptures opens the way for us to receive the interior revelation of Jesus Christ, the Son of Man and the Son of God.

To engage with theosis, requires our profound encounter with the grand salvation history described in the kerygma of God's plan from the foundation of the earth: Creation, the Fall, the Re-Creation, and our response to this plan. Mary exemplifies the correct response to the kerygma as she studied and pondered the Scriptures understanding this incredible plan that God wants to restore us. Original Sin causes the great divorce and leads to hellish suffering, including eternal death. Her example inspires us to ponder these same scriptures to conquer sin, death, and the cause, Lucifer, so we may be glorified in Christ.

All may engage with this great mystical and spiritual journey because within our hearts lies our yearning for holiness and the encounter with God. Vatican II with its adoption of Aquinas' scriptural interpretations and of new understandings of the Church Fathers helped open this encounter for the Beatific Vision to us. Bishop Barron states that the Council believed that its "recovery of the more lyrical language of the early Church Fathers and of the Scriptures . . . would facilitate the process of bringing the light of Christ to the men and women of our time."[9] The spiritual regeneration caused by Vatican II encourages us on the search for the Beatific Vision. This participation in living holiness calls us to seek through theosis the Face of God, Father, Son, and Holy Spirit.

---

9. Barron, *Vatican II Collection*, x.

SECTION ONE

Seeking the Face of God the Father

Chapter One

THE POWER OF THE WORD

"Seek the Face of God! Hide not your face from me, Oh God."
—PSALM 27:8

ST. JOHN PAUL II experienced the horrors of World War II as he watched the occupation and destruction of his homeland, Poland. He watched his entire family die, and he went underground to study to become a priest. Working in a factory, he knew the fatigues of physical labor. Yet when he became pope, he strode out on the Vatican balcony with courage proclaiming, "Do not be afraid!"

How could this be? St. John Paul II knew the worldly reasons for fear and how quickly evil can take over. He had watched evil enter. He had lived the reality of evil. He understood the spiritual despair which gripped the hearts and souls of many, yet he stood with courage and conviction, trusting in the presence of God. For St. John Paul II had also lived the great spiritual adventure and journey of participation in God, called theosis or divinization. He knew that Jesus Christ infuses his perfect goodness within us, calling us to newness of the Spirit, a movement St. John Paul II later called the New Pentecost: the infusion of divine love in the soul. In this perennial event, the New Pentecost enlivens the mystical body of Christ, calling all Christians to seek perfection.

3

In St. John Paul II's theology, we see the key to his faith: a profound belief in human perfectibility through theosis, the growth of divinity within the human being. St. John Paul II lived his theories and preached this New Pentecost followed by the New Evangelization. While we understand the historical significance of his life as a leader, St. John Paul II's theology of theosis in the New Pentecost, God's gift of divine love and promotion of this through a New Evangelization leading to the Beatific Vision, still needs a fresh exploration and understanding for Christian theology. Theosis offers a rich, personal, and practiced experience within Christianity.

The New Pentecost gives us hope for our perfection and union with God. We spend our lives seeking fulfillment of many desires yet still experience discontent. We desire material satisfaction, along with love and meaning. Yet none of us find fulfillment without engaging in a search that requires the transcendence of our lives, heart, mind, and soul. We hunger for the sight of our Divine Artisan, Creator, for whom we are made. Our passion to see God's face calls to us. St. John Paul II emphasizes the importance of beauty for us. St. Francis of Assisi saw his Divine Artisan after receiving the stigmata, crying out, "You are beauty!" Commenting on St. Francis' mystical experience of divine love being infused into his soul, St. Bonaventure writes: "In things of beauty, he contemplated the One who is supremely beautiful, and, led by the footprints he found in creatures, he followed the Beloved everywhere."[1] This divine beauty lingers in our consciousness, becomes the source of our prayers, and at times of blessing, touches our very soul.

Why seek the Face of the Father and the divine essence? Without God, the source of all love, we are empty of both divine and human love. God alone completes and satisfies every passion and desire as we long to see his face. In his dissertation. John Paul defines the essence of divinity, writing, "the intellect attains to the very essence of divinity and enjoys its presence in a clear manner."[2]

This fulfillment St. John Paul II calls *Communio Personarum*. The Face of the Father offers a hidden place for our completion in the Kingdom of Heaven. In *Communio* we enjoy intimacy heart-to-heart with the divine, fulfilling our desire to belong to another forever face to face. *Communio Personarum*, then, is an eternal exchange of love between God and humanity.

1. John Paul II, *Artists*, sec. 6.
2. John Paul II, *Faith*, 81.

St. Augustine in his *The Trinity* describes the danger of not seeking the face of God. We live in carelessness if we do not passionately seek the Face of God. Our temptations increasing, we want to be like God divided from God, and then descend to the path of failure—rebellion—which ends in us becoming like beasts. Our distorted appetites make us act like a snake carelessly gliding along on its scales, wriggling through various human experiences, tasting everything with delight, then squeezing life out of other persons. We become tempted to prove our own power, as Adam and Eve did, and this desire expands into the temptation to be like God, deciding good and evil for ourselves. Seeking human power instead of divine wisdom, our envy and greed lead us to claim and prove our own empowerment. We think, "Nobody can rule over me, not even God!" Hence, my will and way reigns over God's will and way. We choose to divorce ourselves from God, indulging our desires until we are gorged with narcissism. We then strip ourselves naked of our first robes of *imago dei* and divine dignity to put on the skins of mortality, being made in the likeness of the snake. This is Original Sin!

Our love disappears. Knowledge puffs us up (1 Cor 8:1). Augustine captures this unfortunate human feeling aptly, writing, "Consciousness is overweighted with a sort of self-heaviness and is therefore heaved out of happiness."[3] God's punishment allows us to indulge freely and completely in our unhealthy passions and we become beast-like, rabid for pride and pleasure, yet bereft of happiness. Psalm 49:12 describes this, "Man established in honor did not understand; he was matched with senseless cattle and became like them." In this form of humanity, we live in misery, while committing evil. Made a little lower than the angels, we have become less than a snake. In profound despair, we become tormented by the sight of our loss. Augustine describes this horror. "It learns to its punishment what a difference there is between the good it has forsaken and the evil it has committed; nor can it go back up again, having squandered and lost its strength, except by the grace of its maker calling it to repentance and forgiving his sins."[4]

Yet our torment at forsaking goodness may bring us to see God's healing restoration. Through seeking the Face of God, we may heal from this self-destructive fall for his embrace reclothes us in divine grace. Augustine writes, "For man's true honor is God's image and likeness in him, but it can

3. Augustine, *Trinity*, 331.

4. Augustine, *Trinity*, 331.

only be preserved when facing him from whom its likeness is received."[5] Keeping our love alive, facing God the Father, keeps and preserves in us the *imago dei*: We are made in the image of God—not a snake!

To keep our image of God alive is described in St. John Paul II's *Communio Personarum*. In his doctoral dissertation, St. John Paul II speaks of *Communio Personarum* as a participation in the Divine Life: *Dios par participation*. Our participation is an essential communion in the Divine— God's essence is love and so our nature is not just to love, but to fulfill the command to become perfect in love. Pentecost perfects our love, not idolizing ourselves or worshiping some pagan god, but knowing we are adopted by the Father to experience his presence and a heart relating completely, intimately, and personally with another: Himself.

We cultivate *Communio Personarum* by our free will. In this insight, God absolutely respects our free-will, empowers me to become fully human for I am made to love and can only love what I know freely. My choice to essentially participate in the *Communio Personarum* perfects me. It is the ultimate pearl, that Jesus tells us to sell everything once we have found that which we seek. Jesus himself invites us into this participation as he longed to eat that Passover Meal with his disciples. He still longs to live with us, sanctifying us, for his dwelling place is with us (Rev 21:3).

THEOSIS: WHAT IS LOVE?

The early Church Fathers recognized the glories of our participation in God and a growing sense of theosis. St. Augustine describes this new state of divine grace originating from the New Pentecost. He proclaims, "Anyone, therefore, who has learned to love the new life has learned to sing a new song, and the new song reminds us of our new life. The new man, the new song, the new covenant, all belong to the one kingdom of God, and so the new man will sing a new song and will belong to the new covenant."[6]

What is this new joyful love? This power changes the face of the world, sings in our hearts, and spiritually enlivens the soul. Love completes our heart. But from where does love come? St. Augustine continues addressing this perplexing question.

---

5. Augustine, *Trinity*, 331.

6. Augustine, *Let Us Sing*.

The psalms do not tell us not to love, but to choose the object of our love. But how can we choose unless we are first chosen? We cannot love unless someone has loved us first. Listen to the apostle John: We love him because he first loved us. The source of man's love for God can only be found in the fact that God loved him first. He has given us himself as the object of our love, and he has also given us its source.[7]

In theosis, as St. Augustine reveals, we are chosen by God. Created in love for love, we may live in the covenant of love which the whole of creation expresses in all its beauty and splendor. God's love creates and completes us healing our subjectivity and self-determination, showing we cannot love perfectly—our ultimate desire—unless shown first perfect love. "Finding us in a state of deformity, the Spirit restores our original beauty and fills us with his grace, leaving no room for anything unworthy of our love."[8]

Our exterior life, as seen in the structure of our world and universe, battles for prominence with our interior life, that is our relationship with God. Yet our interior life communicates the divine. Our interior search yearns for an explanation of who we are in this world. In this craving, the unfathomable happens: "God created man in his own image, in the image of God he created him; male and female he created them" (Gen 1:27). Commenting on this passage, Maximus the Confessor (580–662 CE), a man who lived theosis, explains this. In the incarnation, God "makes man god to the same degree as God Himself became man" except that he "will divinize human nature without changing it into the divine nature."[9]

DESIRING *COMMUNIO PERSONARUM*

The Spirit breathes and the very breath of God emanates divinity and aspires to create pure beauty. We become commingled, uniting with God. St. John Paul II uses the analogy of a pure marriage to describe this. Nothing more beautiful exists than man and woman free, fruitful, and full of grace who commingle their hearts becoming one with the other, though always two. Their marital union discloses our created beauty, gifting love to the other in mutual participation in Divine Love. St. John Paul II uses nuptial love, gift-love, to explain created *communio*.

7. Augustine, *Let Us Sing*.
8. Didymus, *Treatise*, 667.
9. Maximus, *Various Texts on Theology*, sec. 62, under "First Century."

Marriage reflects *Communio Personarum* as husband and wife gift themselves to each other as do the Three Persons of the Trinity. Partaking of gift love leads to theosis.

Just as two people are joined together in one flesh, all the while maintaining the integrity of their separate identities, just as they share a single existence and hold all things in common, so the believer is joined to God in an ineffable communion (cf. 1 Cor 6:15–17).

This is theosis, the way to the Uncreated *Communio Personarum*! God invites us to partake in God's life which as the scriptures tell us is love. "God is love, and whoever abides in love abides in God, and God abides in him" (1 John 4:16). To abide in love, prayer opens our heart to become one with our Beloved. *Lectio Divina* teaches us to pray as God wills, not as we want. This contemplative prayer first conforms and then unites our will to the Divine will. Becoming one with Divine Love, we sing this hymn at the elevation of the Eucharist in the Maronite Divine Liturgy.

> You have united O Lord,
> your divinity with our humanity,
> and our humanity with your divinity;
> your life with our mortality
> and our mortality with your life.
> You have assumed what is ours
> and you have given us what is yours,
> for the life and salvation of our souls.
> To you be glory forever.[10]

Participating in the Divine Nature causes many modern-day Christians pause. Do we become one with God? Is everything created God: Pantheism? Is everything identified in God: Panentheism? Do we compromise and claim human nature to be equal to the divine nature? Rooted in biblical beliefs concerning the origins of man, Jesus clearly states we are divine creatures.

> Is it not written in your Law, "I said, you are gods"? If he called them gods to whom the word of God came—and Scripture cannot be broken—do you say of him whom the Father consecrated and sent into the world, "You are blaspheming," because I said, "I am the Son of God"? (John 10:34)

---

10. Ghosn, *The Maronite Divine Liturgy of St. James.*

We are the *imago dei*, the image of God, as St. Paul commands: "Be renewed in the spirit of your minds, and to put on the new self, created after the likeness of God in true righteousness and holiness" (Eph 4:23–24).

God glorifies us, his created creatures, transforming us by his grace which is the infusion of his life into our fallen human nature. We become a new creation—born again through water and the Spirit—for we have a new life in Christ. We do not lose our creaturely nature—limited and finite—but we are perfected, fully human through divine participation.

St. Gregory of Nyssa captures this insight into divine participation, as did so many Greek Fathers of the early Church. We "possess the image of God by being rational; you receive the likeness of God by acquiring virtue. In creation I have the image, but I become through the exercise of my free will in the likeness of God."[11] Partaking in the Divine is a choice of our free-will to either put on the new life of Christ, or stay fallen, divorced from the covenant God offers all. This divinizing grace is ours to choose.

Theosis makes us choose; it participates, partakes, and communicates who we are in Christ. Or as St. Peter who experienced this divinization explains.

> His divine power has granted to us all things that pertain to life and godliness, through the knowledge of him who called us to his own glory and excellence, by which he has granted to us his precious and very great promises, so that through them you may become *partakers of the divine nature*, having escaped from the corruption that is in the world because of sinful desire. (2 Pet 1:3–4; italics added)

The divine essence that Jesus reveals at his Transfiguration and Ascension, we too experience in our theosis. Through *Lectio Divina*, we experience a transfiguration and ascension ourselves. This belongs to the essence of our human nature, not that we become equal to the uncreated Divine Nature, but we commingle with the Divine as St. Irenaeus says.

> It is manifest, too, that God has the power to confer life upon it, inasmuch as He grants life to us who are in existence. And, therefore, since the Lord has power to infuse life into what He fashioned, and since the flesh is capable of being quickened, what remains to prevent its participating in incorruption, which is the blissful and never-ending life granted by God?[12]

11. Quoted in Nicodemus, *Handbook*, 219.
12. Irenaeus, *Against Heresies*, 5.3.3.

YEARNING FOR BEAUTY: PHILOKALIA

Philokalia, a term used by the Greek Fathers to express love of the beautiful, is bliss. St. John Paul II calls this the inscrutable image of Divine Beauty, which reveals our spiritual integrity, a wholeness in which clarity, harmony, and radiance all converge. We become one with God, not as Father and Son, but as adopted sons and daughters, abiding in the will of God.

> Beloved, if our heart does not condemn us, we have confidence before God; and whatever we ask we receive from him, because we keep his commandments and do what pleases him. And this is his commandment, that we believe in the name of his Son Jesus Christ and love one another, just as he has commanded us. Whoever keeps his commandments abides in God, and God in him. And by this we know that he abides in us, by the Spirit whom he has given us. (1 John 3:21–24)

St. John Paul II shows us the journey toward the Face of the Father and the glories of the Beatific Vision. Through our faith which St. John Paul II understood as participation in experiential and practical knowledge, we glimpse the Beatific Vision. He writes in his dissertation how our faith connects us with God.

> The essence shared by faith and divinity converge and forge an intentional identification of the human subject and the divine object. The likeness is on the intellectual level then; it is reason that is intimately united to God in faith. Faith operates within the mind and fosters a direct contact with God. John of the Cross frequently compares faith as essentially the same as beatific vision—one sees God. But faith's sight is insufficient for the intellect never fully comprehends God in faith; it assents to him.[13]

Through the *communio personarum*, St. John Paul II states we make the gift of self to others. Indeed, desiring the breadth of the *imago dei* begins our transformation into this living and generous gift, beatification. This theistic humanism rooted in the New Pentecost proclaims, "I become a gift because I receive the only gift of value, the Spirit of Divine Love the *Communio Personarum*." This took place at the first Pentecost and continues forever, for we are a Pentecostal people living daily in this new Spirit evangelizing that we love because Infinite Love, the *Communio Personarum* loves us.

13. John Paul II, *Faith*, 92.

THE PROCLAMATION OF THE HOLY SPIRIT BY THE SECOND VATICAN COUNCIL

St. John XXIII emphasized the work of the Holy Spirit in his opening address for the Second Vatican Council.

> We must recognize here the hand of God, who, as the years roll by, is ever directing men's efforts, whether they realize it or not, towards the fulfillment of the inscrutable designs of His providence, wisely arranging everything, even adverse human fortune, for the Church's good.[14]

The Second Vatican Council affirms the power and presence of the mysterious work of redemption that inspires the Church and the faithful to fully participate in the Body of Christ using our Pentecostal gifts. These gifts are given for one purpose to increase our Sacred Worship: the adoration of our God. Pope Benedict offers a simple hermeneutic of the word adoration, mouth to mouth, or as the Song of Songs tells us, "Let him kiss me with the kisses of his mouth!" (Song 1:2). Authentic Sacred Worship expands our union with the Father and is the essence of the Second Vatican Council's renewal. As then Cardinal Ratzinger defines, "The Church stands or falls with the Liturgy. The true celebration of the sacred liturgy is at the center of any renewal of the Church."[15]

Vatican II emphasized the Holy Spirit in different ways, as Pope Paul VI states.

> It is known to all how the Council has filled the pages of its sublime and very topical teachings with continuous mentions of the Holy Spirit. There are those who have counted 258. Let us make ours the multiple exhortation of the Council, and we put at the preface of our Holy Year the repeated and ever new invocation: Come, O Holy Spirit; come, O Creator Spirit; come, O Spirit Comforter![16]

In 1975, Pope Paul VI summarized Vatican II, saying, "Assuredly we have here a work of the Spirit, a gift of Pentecost."[17]

Why did the Church in her great wisdom emphasize the gifts of the Holy Spirit? The Holocaust and genocide brought the horrors of human

---

14. John XXIII, "Opening Address," 4–5.
15. Quoted in Mattei, "Reflections on the Liturgical Reform," 141.
16. Paul VI, "General Audience, May 23, 1973."
17. Paul VI, *Gaudete in Domino*.

degradation, while destroying—annihilating—the very concept of who and what a human being is. Because of this, our recent popes have emphasized the need for the active experience of the Holy Spirit in the church and for the gifts of the Holy Spirit. In an address to ecclesial movements and new communities, St. John Paul II stated: "The institutional and charismatic aspects are co-essential . . . to the Church's constitution. . . . Today, I would like to cry out to all of you gathered here in St. Peter's Square and to all Christians: Open yourselves docilely to the gifts of the Spirit! Accept gratefully and obediently the charisms which the Spirit never ceases to bestow on us!"[18]

St. Paul VI also saw this great danger and dire peril in the 20th century as he witnessed the self-destruction of humanity. In response, he prayed for an outpouring of the Creating Spirit of God.

> Not that Pentecost has ever ceased to be an actuality during the whole history of the Church, but so great are the needs and the perils of the present age, so vast the horizon of mankind drawn towards world coexistence and powerless to achieve it, that there is no salvation for it except in a new outpouring of the gift of God. Let Him then come, the Creating Spirit, to renew the face of the earth!"[19]

The Second Vatican Council powerfully responded to traumatized and suffering humanity's profound needs after the twentieth century's murderous wars. We want peace, not war. We want harmony, not conflicts. We want healing, not another war, was the mentality of those in the 1950s, yet the unrest, conflicts, and the gaping wounds were growing. Pope John XXIII describes his prayerful reaction to this.

> What should the Church do? Should Christ's mystical barque simply drift along, tossed this way and that by the ebb and flow of the tides? Or is she not instead expected not simply to issue a new warning, but to offer also the light of a great example? What could that light be? My interlocutor listened with reverence and attention. Suddenly, my soul was illumined by a great idea which came precisely at that moment and which I welcomed with ineffable confidence in the divine Teacher. And there sprang to my lips

---

18. John Paul II, "Ecclesial Movements," sec. 4–5.

19. Paul VI, *Gaudete in Domino.*

a word that was solemn and committing. My voice uttered it for the first time: "A Council!"[20]

Pope John XXIII said the idea of the council appeared as "a spontaneous flower of an unexpected spring."[21] And so the idea and reality of an ecumenical council began with the prayerful exploration of renewal, spiritual gifts, of indeed a New Pentecost, a cleansing and healing after mass genocide. To this end, the Council produced rich and rewarding documents. Among spiritual disciplines introduced were the ancient practices of *Lectio Divina* and theosis, contemplating the Holy Spirit, bringing perfection of soul through dwelling in the Trinity.

How does spiritual renewal happen? Through a willingness to suffer in faith "for the sake of Christ you should not only believe in him but also suffer for his sake" (Phil 1:29). Through our suffering, we may find not only intimacy but union with God. This path toward union is called theosis, that Greek term, moving us toward a close, intimate communion with God. St. John Paul II writes, "Man becomes the image of God not so much in the moment of solitude as in the moment of communion. Right "from the beginning, he is not only an image in which the solitude of a person who rules the world is reflected, but also, and essentially, an image of an inscrutable divine communion of persons."[22]

Theosis purifies us, gradually revealing the glory of God, the Beatific Vision in which we see the essence of who we are for we see who made us: Love himself. Our dwelling place beholds the transcendent beauty, glory, and majesty of God, for he does not merely lift us up—transfigures us— He also humbles himself to become one with us. United, we are divinized. With pure humility and hope our humble efforts here awaken our innate desire to enter this journey, to find the Way. "Come and see," Jesus invites us into his life (John 1:39). He is the Way and the Catholic Church with her long, rich history rooted in apostolic tradition continues to pave this path to theosis.

Sadly, in our day, we struggle to express these lofty ideas simply, practically, and experientially. Conflicting interpretations of the Second Vatican Council introduce unrest and plague our history now with many divisions concerning the fruits of the council. Yet instead of arguing and quarrelling, the Spirit inspires us to explore and experience the power and presence of

20. Komonchak, "Ecumenical Council," 4.
21. Komonchak, "Ecumenical Council," 4.
22. John Paul II, *Communion of Persons*.

the Spirit working in the Church and individuals, so we can heal, renew, and change the face of the Church.

The coming chapters present a way to theosis, the Truth of Jesus, Who offers us new life, a life in the Spirit, as lived by those great mystics: Rebekah, the matriarch of the covenant; Mary, the Spouse of the Holy Spirit; Jacob who beheld the Face of the Father; Guigo and his mystical Ladder; St. Bernard of Clairvaux, the humble mystic; St. Thomas Aquinas, the Angelic Doctor; St. John of the Cross, the divine mystic; St. Maximillian Kolbe, the martyr of love; St. John Paul II, the author of the New Evangelization; and of course the Catholic Church with her magisterial role. The Church, built by these living stones, all reveal as in a prism, different glimpses of Love, inviting us to embrace the Way, the Truth, and Life in which we ought to partake. The hope of theosis is breathtaking: Jesus Christ takes our very being and tests us to live a life of theosis, abiding within the beauty, power and glory of the Trinity, Father, Son, and Holy Spirit.

Chapter Two

SACRED SCRIPTURE
Mirroring Our God

THE MYSTICAL MEANING OF SCRIPTURE

How DO WE BEGIN theosis, the most amazing of all human interior journeys? The full interpretation of scripture guides us in seeking theosis. In wisdom, we read and understand Sacred Scripture based on Thomas Aquinas' four-fold method of literal and mystical scriptural interpretations. These transcendent meanings purify our very hearts in preparation for the Beatific Vision.

One of Vatican's II great contributions was the emphasis on the literal and mystical interpretation of scripture. St. John Paul II officially interpreted scriptures through the great patristic fathers who unveiled these understandings of the Sacred Word as interpreted by the Roman Catholic Church. The words and stories of scripture are seamless, enlightening us on this path to theosis. The Magisterium or the official teaching authority of the Church understands Sacred Scripture within the Sacred Tradition. She also understands the Old and New Testament as an historical and unified whole, "a mirror in which the pilgrim Church on earth looks at God, from whom she has received everything, until she is brought finally to see Him as He is, face to face (see 1 John 3:2)."[1] The Catholic Catechism, quoting from Vatican II's document *Dei Verbum* paragraphs 7–10, states: "Sacred

---

1. Paul VI, *Dei Verbum*, sec. 7.

Tradition and Sacred Scripture, then, are bound closely together, and communicate one with the other. For both of them, flowing out from the same divine well-spring, come together in some fashion to form one thing, and move towards the same goal. Each of them makes present and fruitful in the Church the mystery of Christ, who promised to remain with his own "always, to the close of the age."[2]

Vatican II's *Dei Verbum*, a document St. John Paul II, Joseph Ratzinger (Pope Benedict XVI), Hans urs Van Balthasar, and Henri du Lubac helped write, influenced the direction of the council and called for a renewal of scripture studies in light of early Christian commentaries called Patristics. The church fathers—Patristics—revealed the spiritual and mystical meanings of scripture hidden within the literal understanding, as the Second Vatican Council discerns:

> The bride of the incarnate Word, the Church taught by the Holy Spirit, is concerned to move ahead toward a deeper understanding of the Sacred Scriptures so that she may increasingly feed her sons with the divine words. Therefore, she also encourages the study of the holy Fathers of both East and West and of sacred liturgies.[3]

The divine words reveal Christ as the Bridegroom, the focus and fulfilment of Sacred Scripture. This nuptial image threads itself throughout the Old and New Testament and finds fulfillment in the promised marriage between the Divinity and humanity of Christ as the Bridegroom and his Church. Divinity unites himself with our humanity for God wanted to be one with his people. This is the mystery of the incarnation for God throughout the Old and New Testaments uses this nuptial theme to create this union.

To create this closeness, the scriptures woo us into a conversation in which the Bridegroom reveals his thirst for our love. This is the great mystery of the Wedding Feast at Cana; the Word of God longs for us! The prophets of the Old Testament prepare us to understand this hour—consummation of love. God speaks to his people first through the inspired Word written by human authors, then through the Son speaking to us directly, inviting us into a deep, intimate, face to face conversation. In so doing, we see ourselves not as an insignificant creature, but as a person worthy of his love.

2. *Catechism*, sec. 80.

3. Paul VI, *Dei Verbum*, sec. 23.

> Long ago, at many times and in many ways, God spoke to our fa-
> thers by the prophets, but in these last days he has spoken to us by
> his Son, whom he appointed the heir of all things, through whom
> also he created the world. He is the radiance of the glory of God
> and the exact imprint of his nature, and he upholds the universe
> by the word of his power. After making purification for sins, he sat
> down at the right hand of the Majesty on high. (Heb 1:1–3).

Twenty-five years after the Second Vatican Council in his address commemorating *Dei Verbum*, St. John Paul II comments on the power of Sacred Scripture: God speaking to us his family as sons and daughters worthy of his love because of his unconditional love for us.

> The opening phrase *Dei Verbum*, which serves as the title of the
> document, is not, as people are sometimes tempted to think, a
> mere synonym for "Sacred Scripture." Its meaning is much broad-
> er and more comprehensive; it signifies the living Word of God as
> God continually communicates it to the Church and through the
> Church, so as to awaken faith and lead people into a life of com-
> munion with one another and with God. Written words alone do
> not suffice for the transmission of this living and life-giving Word.
> They must be carried along by a current of life that animates them,
> namely, the current of the great Tradition, which, docile to the
> Holy Spirit places every text in its true light and makes it bear fruit.
> The Church's Teaching Office is at the service of this transmission,
> whose fidelity it guarantees in accordance with God's will.[4]

LECTIO DIVINA

St. John Paul II testifies to the "living and life-giving Word" refreshing our soul. Yet how do we receive the living Word? One of the most biblically centered methods of reading and interpreting scripture leading to theosis comes to us from the Carthusian Monk named Guigo (1140–93). Working and laboring as monks do, God spoke to him revealing that Jacob's Ladder is the stairway to heaven, the way to theosis (see Gen 28:10–17). This ladder symbolically represents Guigo's method of Biblical interpretation called *Lectio Divina*. This ladder has four steps of reading, meditation, prayer, and contemplation which unveils the way to seek the Face of the Father. These steps prepare and infuse the Spirit so we may behold and understand the

---

4. Béchard, *Scripture Documents*, 164.

Word of God, Jesus Christ who stands atop of the ladder (2 Cor 4:6). "May He lead us from virtue to virtue, up to the top of the mysterious ladder, into the vision of God in Zion."[5]

In *Lectio Divina*, we apply our hearts and minds to seek these hidden, mysterious truths in the vision of God. As we do this, they transform through a catharsis purifying from within. Now reconciled to God, we become temples of the Holy Spirit perfected by his presence dwelling within. We seek the everlasting joy of the divine presence in our souls: the gift of God's Spirit filling the sails of our soul.

In *Lectio Divina*, we ascend toward this Beatific Vision seen in God dwelling in the New Jerusalem. Our souls rejoice in the profound knowledge of God the Father who gives us everything we need to fully partake of his blessings: to dwell in the Holy Spirit. In *lectio*, we touch the three transcendentals of eternal truth, goodness, and beauty, captivating our mind, memory, and heart. Knowing these three transcendentals, we experience, encounter, and finally commune with God, called by St. John Paul II the *Communio Personarum*. What does the Father give to us in *Communio Personarum?* Himself, eternal love! We tremble at the magnitude of this great gift—and in our awe, we fall down and worship.

Through *Lectio Divina*, we discern the transcendent path of theosis. Living under the evil governments of Nazism and Communism, St. John Paul II hungered his whole life for the transcendent. The Sacred Mysteries revealed in Sacred Scripture fortified his soul. He strengthened himself with the truth, goodness, and beauty of this mysterious God. St. John Paul II describes Sacred Scripture as a "sort of 'immense vocabulary' (Paul Claudel) and 'iconographic atlas' (Marc Chagall), from which both Christian culture and art have drawn. . . . But for everyone, believers or not, the works of art inspired by Scripture remain a reflection of the unfathomable mystery which engulfs and inhabits the world."[6]

God is the Divine Artisan. Mystics and artists penetrate these divine mysteries hidden within creation and scriptures. Artists uncover them in pictures, paintings, sculptures, poetry, literature, and songs. When we apprehend divine beauty, the most attractive of the transcendentals, we look and yearn for more. Beauty stops us in our tracks and takes our breath away. In divine beauty, we find the reality scripture describes: "Be still and know

---

5. Guigo, *Ladder*, 8.

6. John Paul II, *Artists*, 5.

that I am God" (Ps 46:10). Our stillness makes us delve deeper into the unfathomable mysteries revealed to us through this perennial Pentecost.

Guigo describes his method as the means to satisfy our hunger for the transcendent place where God, Father, Son, and Holy Spirit dwells. In our *lectio*, ultimately, we commune and comingle with the divine presence in our soul as his dwelling place, the ultimate purpose of theosis.

A *LECTIO DIVINA*: OUR FATHER

Our Father: My identity comes from you and my essence is in you. I can never escape my identity with you.

Who art in heaven: Where the river of life flows and where I will be consummated one day. The blood and water which flowed out of the side of the Jesus on the cross flows in heaven. I need not fear the unveiling of the apocalypse.

Hallowed be thy name: The glory of God the Shekinah shines around your name and you give your beautiful radiance to us.

Thy kingdom come: With the beauty of a pearl within me connecting me to the community of the Kingdom of God already—a world full of activity and communion.

Thy will be done: All you have is ours! Your will is my home and you are my Divine Confidant.

On earth as it is in heaven: In this world the Fall has destroyed us and you came to conquer sin and the source of sin within the world and give me a new life of metanoia.

Give us this day: We are to ask from you as a Father who longs to give us good things. The universe is created with the identity of Fatherhood.

Our daily bread: When we eat the Eucharist, we are transformed, and our souls unite with you.

Lead us not into temptation: Of thinking that we can make wise or good decisions without you. Of listening to the insinuating thoughts of the demon.

But deliver us from evil: God's goodness not only protects us from evil and from the Evil One, but also restores the goodness in us lost by Adam's sin.

AQUINAS' FOUNDATIONAL METHOD OF BIBLICAL INTERPRETATION

St. John Paul II speaks of the rich life and actions that we have on our way to union with God. His phrases still echo in our consciousness: The New Evangelization, the New Pentecost. Jesus Christ says, "Behold, I make all things new" (Rev 21:5). Where does this newness come from? The method of *Lectio Divina* introduces the hidden meanings in Sacred Scripture, using Aquinas' simple formula of the interpretation. The practice of *Lectio Divina* along with the theology of Aquinas unite to make a trustworthy way to the Beatific Vision.

Aquinas, who exemplifies theosis, reveals in his great work the *Summa Theologica*, that the literal and foundational sense of scripture must be understood correctly. Yet, within the literal sense are these other senses: the allegorical sense which reveals to us Christ and his mission; the tropological sense, or moral sense, revealing to us how we are to become righteous in the eyes of our Father; and the anagogical sense or purpose of scripture which reveals to us the glories of heaven, our destiny and ultimate goal: sanctification.[7]

In explanation of Aquinas' scriptural interpretation, the Catholic Catechism quotes the medieval pithy explanation: "The Letter speaks of deeds; Allegory to faith; The Moral how to act; Anagogy our destiny."[8] This concise couplet summarizes St. Thomas' complicated explanation in the *Summa Theologica* which responds to the question: Whether in Holy Scripture a word may have several senses?

> Therefore that first signification whereby words signify things belongs to the first sense, the historical or literal. That signification whereby things signified by words have themselves also a signification is called the spiritual sense, which is based on the literal, and presupposes it. Now this spiritual sense has a threefold division. For as the Apostle says (Hebrews 10:1) the Old Law is a figure of the New Law, and Dionysius says (Coel. Hier. i) "the New Law itself is a figure of future glory." Again, in the New Law, whatever our Head has done is a type of what we ought to do. Therefore, so far as the things of the Old Law signify the things of the New Law, there is the allegorical sense; so far as the things done in Christ, or so far as the things which signify Christ, are types of what we

7. Aquinas, *Summa Theologica*, I.1.10; *Catechism*, sec. 115–19.

8. *Catechism*, sec. 118.

ought to do, there is the moral sense. But so far as they signify
what relates to eternal glory, there is the anagogical sense.[9]

In brief, then, this scriptural interpretation offers us fruitful faith,
moral actions, and eternal fulfillment for they reveal an involved and powerful path to the vision of the Face of the Father. We read the literal level
first with real facts, thoughts, and actions in which we hear of historical
activities and powerful destinies. Yet, scripture rooted in the literal sense
also contains signs, symbols, and types to expose parallels and other meanings hidden within the characters and personalities. Aquinas teaches that
sometimes all four senses come into play while studying passages within
the scriptures and at other times it may only be three, two, or just one sense.

More than just narratives, history, poetry, psalms, proverbs, and stories, scriptures reveal the Divine Logos, Jesus Christ. The perfection of the
Word, the Logos made flesh, creates within us a new and refreshed soul, a
powerful vision of God within our heart, nuptial bliss in the Kingdom of
God.

Some people, however, tend to read Scripture with their own mind set,
rather than trying to read scripture from the mindset in which it was written. Someone who studies ancient manuscripts but reads them with a 21st
century mindset struggles to grasp the nuances and symbols represented in
the manuscript as well as the culture or the customs of the ancients. Aquinas' scriptural typology includes the literal sense, the historical backdrop in
customs and cultures in which these sacred writings were written, as well as
the spiritual and mystical interpretation we ought to perceive. These profound scriptural insights into the mysteries bless us with understanding.

St. John Paul II recognizes that the Old Testament contains pre-figu-
rations that are only understood and fulfilled in the New Testament for the
New Testament completes the Old Testament. Typology penetrates those
hidden, mystical meanings contained in the figures, characteristics, and
stories of the Old Testament prefigure and fulfill the New Testament teachings of Jesus, giving profound contextual understanding as to why Jesus
does what he does.

Typology understands the Old Testament as the foundation pointing
to fulfillment in the New Testament. Indeed, Augustine says that the Old
Testament is the hidden and concealed version of the New Testament; and
the New Testament reveals the fullness of God at the capacity of man's ability to understand.

9. Aquinas, *Summa Theologica*, I.1.10.

Typology gives a richer, deeper, and fuller sense of the meanings of the Word when applied correctly, so we can reflect on the first creation and its Fall from *Communio Personarum*. Before the Fall, we walked hand in hand with our God. The rest of the Old Testament reveals God's plan for restoration: a re-Creation through the Spirit so we again can walk hand and hand with God in the New Jerusalem. Delving into the mysteries of the new creation, the New Testament reveals the restoration of theosis in the New Pentecost: the anagogical purpose of the New Testament.

> The Word became flesh to make us "partakers of the divine nature": "For this is why the Word became man, and the Son of God became the Son of man: so that man, by entering into communion with the Word and thus receiving divine sonship, might become a son of God." "For the Son of God became man so that we might become God." "The only-begotten Son of God, wanting to make us sharers in his divinity, assumed our nature, so that he, made man, might make men gods."[10]

Thus, the Old Testament slowly reveals who God is and his foundational plan for salvation, so that we, who are living in the New Covenant, the New Testament, the fulfillment of *Communio Personarum*, may recognize more and more of the Lord to perceive who this Lord really is and how we ought to relate to him, seeking the Face of the Father. Our Brother Jesus Christ walks with us up Jacob's Ladder hand in hand, showing us the Face of the Father because he descended the ladder and became one of us.

Aquinas' three transcendentals apply directly to the three spiritual meanings of scripture. The allegorical interpretation reveals the first transcendental, truth: Jesus Christ is God and man. The incarnation of Jesus Christ reveals this truth. The tropological interpretation reveals the second transcendental, goodness. Christ as Goodness himself commands we keep the Law through his grace that makes us good. Finally, the anagogical interpretation reveals the third transcendental, beauty. Christ as the fulfillment and purpose of divine revelation gives the vision of the pure beauty of heaven. In the last transcendental, our Bridegroom Christ calls and then divinizes every person who responds faithfully to his invitation, revealing to them the beautiful, mystical marriage of the wedding feast of the Lamb's Supper, the Kingdom of Heaven.

10. *Catechism*, sec. 460.

In theosis, all three scriptural interpretations and transcendentals unite to call us to the top of the ladder, the Beatific Vision and the divine essence, as Pope Benedict XII reveals in his infallible statement.

> After such intuitive and face-to-face vision and enjoyment has or will have begun for these souls, the same vision and enjoyment has continued and will continue without any interruption and without end until the last Judgment and from then on forever. Divine truth, goodness, and beauty call to our human heart, purifying and preparing our human heart to receive the glories of the divine essence.[11]

How many times has a person read a passage of scripture, meditated, and then prayed for years upon years and then an insight comes never seen before? Through these epiphanies, the Heart of God beautifies our human heart and we hunger for more of this holy encounter. In Guigo's contemplation, the purpose of our *Lectio*, the Logos now prays in us, infusing his thoughts directly in our hearts and minds.

In our contemplative prayer, theosis then takes place, we experience transcendence as St. John Paul II tells artists, "Beauty is a key to the mystery and a call to transcendence."[12] St. Paul also captures theosis when he states that "It is no longer I who live, but He Who lives in me" (Gal 2:20). God, the Spirit, lives and prays within our being.

A PERSONAL REFLECTION: AN UNEXPECTED DEATH

December 21, I went to a college basketball game with my father at the Milwaukee Arena. A graduate of Marquette University and a player on the team in the 1940s, my father was a devoted fan. College sports thrilled our family, especially college basketball. He knew the coaches and trainers on the team and so was intimately connected with Marquette on many levels. Excitement, energy, enthusiasm tempted us every game day for the thrill of victory and agony of defeat was always in the balance. December 22, early that morning, my father died of a heart attack.

From fulfillment to abandonment, my world changed. We went to Mass later that morning and the darkness came. Christmas was hollow.

---

11. Benedict XII, *Benedictus Deus*.

12. John Paul II, *Artists*, sec. 16.

Winter was dark. Friends and neighbors came offering condolences. Weeping and wailing replaced the excitement, energy, and enthusiasm of Christmas. My mother did her best, but her world was shattered. Though she courageously fought through the pain of his death, she suffered deeply the rest of her life.

Every night during prayers for the next year, tears came to us all. What seemed to be a promising season became a total loss, or was it?

St. John Paul II lost his father and cried, "I am so alone!" Death destroys love; it terminates the *communio* and so he as well as me entered the dark night of desolation. Unlike my dark night, his country was destroyed by the Nazi's. His pastors were exterminated; his friends shot without cause. His university was shut down. Religious education, public display of piety, and liturgical celebrations were restricted, seeking to remove God, family, and faith.

St. John Paul II lived an abandoned life, struggling with death, poverty, and persecution daily ever since that fateful day, September 1, 1939, when Germany invaded Poland. Yet, through this total loss of everything he had, he found fulfillment: The Pearl of inestimable value, Jesus Christ. As I faced the death of my father and in reality, the death of my family, somehow I too would find fulfilment. How is that possible?

Each person wrestles with their own evil, persecution, and deception. We have our own personal history filled with emptiness and pain. In this tale of two evils, we suffer both physically and morally. We suffer those who sadly dehumanize our dignity. These woes come as curses, but the curse is a paradox. The curse is actually the remedy to the real pain: *solitudino personarum*, hell itself where I am alone in complete abandonment except the faithful understanding that I was made to live in the glory of God, the *Communio Personarum*. Our *solitudino personarum*—I am so alone—drives us to find consolation in relationships, but not just any relationship. We seek the ultimate relationship, the *Communio Personarum*: beholding the Face of the Father through the Son.

Despite this earthly abandonment, St. John Paul II as well as myself delved deeply into the meaning and purpose of life because the suffering of abandonment—desolation—is so deep. Desolation eats at the human heart for we were made for relationship: created in love, for love; and nothing like the death of a loved one cuts so deeply into the heart of our soul. But in our desolation, we are driven to abandon the darkness and seek the light. In our abandonment, we are desperate for the Light: the *Communio Personarum*.

The darkness of death—the purpose of evil—drives many deeper into the abyss of blackness. Indulging, self-medicating, they escape the blackness momentarily with fleeting pleasures, new possessions, or making powerful alliances all strengthening their earthly escape. In reality, their ego-centric behaviors drive them deeper into the black hole and their addictions and compulsions become controlling magnets solidifying their enslavement. As Dante describes his vision of hell, they become frozen in ice, as Satan himself, whose efforts to free himself by flapping his exposed wings only harden the ice in which he is buried.

The light of the divine *Communio Personarum* draws us out of desolation, as we hear the words from Jesus Christ, "Come and see" (John 1:39).

LECTIO DIVINA: A CHANGE OF IDENTITY GENESIS 18

St. John Paul II exploring theosis talks about the expectation for an inscrutable communion of persons for which we wait and watch. We have an innate yearning for this encounter with God. Our psyches are not closed and hardened when we live in faith seeking the Face of God. God illuminates us with his presence.

Abraham had waited for decades to see the Face of God. Then in the heat of the day, he saw three men on the outskirts standing there (Gen 18). Abraham through faith knew that this was the day of his visitation, the day when the inscrutable communion of the divine persons comes revealing the relationship he had been seeking since he was called to leave the land of Ur.

Abraham runs to them, ecstatic, and implores, "If I have found favor in your sight, do not pass by your servant" (Gen 18:3). His heart touched by the divine knows that these men answer his prayer for *communio*. His heart and being, moved and opened by the Spirit of these three men, finally partakes in their presence.

This is pure theosis in that the Trinity visits his people. Abraham and Sarah receive the revelation that God visits his people and even eats with them. Divine participation begins with a meal, sharing the gift of finest wheat, the bread of angels, and the fruit of the vine.

To relish this invitation to divine friendship Abraham recognizes this visitation as a theophany. He wants to be with them.

To relish this intimate friendship, he asks them to eat with him. First, he invites them to sit under the tree, a place of personal theophany. Abraham offers a morsel of bread to refresh them. With mysterious words revealing their transcendency they declare, "Do as you have said." This strange authority proclaims God's affirmation of Abraham and Sarah's faith to enter the mystery of God's presence. Convicted in faith, Abraham quickly commands Sarah and his servants to prepare a meal, a feast worthy of his God. This morsel of bread quickly multiplies into a banquet.

In the visitation of the three visitors, heaven descends upon Abraham and Sarah as they both behold the Beatific Vision. Both experience the indwelling of Trinity as the three men prophesy that Sarah will conceive and bear a son despite their age and surprise. In their obedience, Abraham and Sarah see the Face of God the Father and received the promise, A son will be given to him and to us.

Re-creation comes in their old age. They had battled the difficulties of faith and doubt, traveling to a far-off land, diverted to Egypt creating marital unrest, questioning the promise of a son, dealing with difficulties within their family, this divine visitation heals and secures the promise. In this visitation, not only do to they celebrate a banquet with their God, have their marriage consummated with a son, and the covenant completed but these all foreshadow the New Covenant, a nuptial marriage, and a heavenly banquet.

This New Covenant multiplies into an everlasting meal in which we too partake in the divine presence, as did Abraham and Sarah. Their morsels of bread and wine foreshadow their Son's Passover Banquet. Jesus, their descendent, took bread, blessed, and then commands us, "Do this in memory of me" (Luke 22:19).

Abraham's obedience to the covenantal sign of circumcision prepares him to recognize the visitation of his God in this theophany of the three men. Because of his obedience, prophetic wonders take place. Sarah conceives. Abraham becomes the father of a multitude whose ultimate offspring is the Son of God, the Son of Abraham. How mysteriously Abraham understands God now, only to enter into the inscrutable fullness of the *Communio Personarum*. The birth of his son, Isaac points to the promise of the Divine Son who completes the real sacrifice of obedience on the Cross. This act is obediential love: God tells Abraham to take his son and offer him as the sacrifice of faith. Abraham becomes our Father in Faith encouraging our own obedience when we too hear the authoritative commands: Do this! Do what, submit our will to God's will as did Abraham.

In theosis then our expectation of a "communion of persons" is met and satisfied through the covenantal obedience.

The authority of God, seen through his covenants, influences our lives. Covenants threaded throughout scripture are everlasting. We still live in the covenant today and will forever. To live in this *Communio Personarum*, we must choose to live the covenant which Sacred Scripture unfolds. This is the typology of scripture study. God reveals himself personally and mysteriously. Theophanies express the inexplicable and inscrutable divine presence that only through faith men and women experience.

In the principal blessing of our lives, we recognize the day of our visitation. God descends into our lives as he did with Abraham and Sarah. This is the anagogical understanding of scripture, revealing their destiny. Abraham, wise in the ways of the Lord, understood who these three were and knows in his heart that they have come to change his life. This is the tropological sense.

In the allegorical sense, the Son of Man, Jesus, invites us to a banquet, a wedding banquet in which he shares himself with us and we give thanks, eucharistasos. Instead of us preparing the banquet, Jesus prepares us through faith to receive the everlasting blessing if we too but circumcise our hearts. When we promise and say I do to those baptismal promises, we as Abraham, as Isaac, as Jacob, become interdependent with our Father who shares with us everything we need. We need grace to keep the covenant and the Father gives us the grace which requires the transformation of our heart, the metanoia, the third step of theosis.

> The kingdom of God announced by Christ can be entered only by a "change of heart" ("metanoia") that is to say through that intimate and total change and renewal of the entire man—of all his opinions, judgments and decisions—which takes place in him in the light of the sanctity and charity of God, the sanctity and charity which were manifested to us in the Son and communicated fully.[13]

When divinity touches us, the Lord's holy presence and fragrance fills us, calling us to respond. When we do say yes, the Lord discloses his soul and heart to us revealing his mysterious actions, remaking our entire self like the two men on the road to Emmaus, Abraham says, "Stay with me for evening is at hand" (Luke 24:29). Our prayer becomes the same. We want to stay in God's presence, in contemplation, and celebrate the everlasting feast together in this meal for we pray: "Show us your face, O Lord" (Ps 27:8).

---

13. Paul VI, *Paenitemini*, sec. 34.

Chapter Three

JACOB'S LADDER

IN OUR SEARCH FOR theosis, we encounter mysteries hidden behind supernatural veils. These transcendental mysteries of truth, goodness, and beauty are revealed to us at the right moment. With meaning enhanced by our *Lectio Divina* on scriptures, these mystical experiences touch our minds and hearts leaving us transformed by the beauty of the divine encounter. Using the Sacred Scriptures' profound history and narratives, we understand how individuals such as Jacob find identity in God and sense how we too can do the same.

The way of theosis, a journey to intimacy with God, begins in our heart-felt desire to seek the face of the Father. We sense a chasm existing between us and God the Father that we cannot cross quickly, though we wish for immediate results. Yet in our consciousness, we sense a ladder and the welcoming invitation, "Come to Me all you who desire me and eat your fill of my fruits" (Sir 24:26). Obedience to God the Father shows us the way and gives us the humility necessary for this spiritual journey.

One of our earliest understandings of the journey to see the Face of the Father comes from the Patriarch Jacob told in Genesis. To see and behold the face of the Father, to climb the ladder to heaven, calls to us as our destiny. To fulfill this, we must choose, as did Jacob, if we want to see the face of God. The key to understanding the struggles we face lies in the "Why" we battle. We toil and labor to find the presence of God; and when we choose to engage in the struggle to find God, God himself will lead us through them—always—if we allow him!

The narrative from the patriarch Jacob and his twin brother Esau reveals our experience in theosis. From the womb, Esau and Jacob struggle with each other for God wants a man with "clean hands and a pure heart" to inherit the blessing of Isaac (Ps 24:4). Esau, however, an earthly man sold his birthright for food, revealing his carnal ways. He also enjoyed and embraced idolatrous Hittite women, causing him to abandon the ways of his God. Seeing this defilement, their mother Rebekah feared the loss of the Covenant and acted.

Standing under the protection of God, Rebekah acted boldly to fulfill Jacob's call to receive Isaac's blessing. She intuits her first-born son Esau to be unworthy of the blessing knowing he would break the covenant as he had sold his birthright. Rebekah, horrified by Esau's spiritual corruption, pleads with Isaac and Jacob. "I loathe my life because of the Hittite women. If Jacob marries one of the Hittite women like these, one of the women of the land, what good will my life be to me?"(Gen 27:46). Spiritually alive, she knows she will die if both her sons marry women worshipping pagan gods for Rebekah's joy came from living in the God of Abraham's Covenant.

Because of her insight, Rebekah, inspired by God-given wisdom, conspires with Jacob into changing Isaac's decision to give the blessing to Esau. Because of this, Isaac blesses Jacob with a permanent blessing. In docility to her wisdom, Jacob submits to the will of his mother, protecting the covenant from Esau's corruption. Jacob then submits a second time to his mother who commands him to leave to avoid his brother's wrath. To continue the covenant, Rebekah, now a woman of foresight, counsels Isaac to command Jacob, "Find a woman of your God, a descendent of my brother Laban, and marry her so together both of you may worship the God of Abraham, Isaac and now yours, the God of Jacob" (Gen 28:1).

On his journey, Jacob has a theophany and, in a dream, sees a ladder with angels ascending and descending on it. The Lord God spoke to him, blessing him as he did Abraham, promising Jacob: "Behold, I am with you and will keep you wherever you go, and will bring you back to this land. For I will not leave you until I have done what I have promised you" (Gen 28:15). Jacob receives and understands this great promise as coming from the Lord. He proclaims this place as the gate of heaven. "Surely the Lord is in this place, and I did not know it." And he was afraid and said, "How awesome is this place! This is none other than the house of God, and this is the gate of heaven" (Gen 28:16–17).

Jacob's dream of a ladder, a stairway, reveals God's design of divine mystery, restoring fallen humanity to divinity. The ladder, a powerful yet practical symbol for all eras, leads to success yet so simple in its design; yet this ladder is different. It does not reach up to heaven; it descends from heaven to be the way up to heaven. In reality, the ladder is Jesus Christ, the Rock upon which God the Father implants and unveils his love.

Jacob sees the Lord standing above allegorically revealing God's plan to descend the ladder to fallen humanity. God enters our condition not to condemn but to raise up. In the descent of the Lord coming down the ladder, his guiding presence makes incredible promises: "The land on which you lie I will give to you and to your offspring. Your offspring shall be like the dust of the earth, and you shall spread abroad to the west and to the east and to the north and to the south, and in you and your offspring shall all the families of the earth be blessed" (Gen 28:13–14).

Jacob accepts and lives within God's promises. Twenty years later, Jacob wrestles with a mysterious man all night and receives a new name. "Your name shall not longer be called Jacob, but Israel, for you have striven with God and with men and have prevailed" (Gen 32:28). Yet, when Jacob asks for the man's name, he received only a blessing, intensifying the revelation of God's presence in his life, saying "For I have seen God face to face, and yet, my life has been delivered" (Gen 32:30).

To ascend the ladder, we use Guigo's method: ascend, be purified, and let the Face of God our Father call, unveil, and bless us. For when we start *Lectio Divina*, that is, begin climbing Jacob's Ladder to seek the Face of the Father, God purifies our heart. We wrestle with God's beauty revealed in creation for only the pure of heart see God. The scriptures reveal the demands that the Word imposes upon us: detachment from this world; and as we read the Word, we wrestle with him and his ways, as did Jacob.

Jacob's Ladder give us insights to help us understand what the Spirit is doing to us on our way to theosis. Yes, we must wrestle with ourselves and with God himself. This struggle of asceticism detaches us from the world of Esau and attaches us to the spirit of Israel.

Through fasting, praying, and doing works of mercy—asceticism— God purifies our hearts as he did Jacob. Catharsis takes place along with a conversion of heart, mind, and spirit leading to metanoia which first changes our thinking and then our hearts. Only through the trials and tests that empty our wills of the self-centered ego-drama do we endure and grow into mystics.

We seek the mystical experience of the uncreated truth, goodness, and beauty of God. Yet we have a choice: which way do we climb the ladder? The ladder not only ascends to heaven, but also descends into the very depths of hell.

On earth, we see the dichotomy. In the material world, we see the sadistic cruelty of humanity wrestling with its own ego as did Esau. Through God's transcendence, we see Jacob wrestling not only with his brother, but also the Angel of God. In his struggle with the Angel, Jacob conquers his ego, humbling himself while asking the Angel for the blessing because he learned meekness through his struggle.

Each person who walks the way of theosis will walk the mystical path of Jacob, experiencing the heavenly delights while seeing the angels of heaven ascending and descending upon us. We will have mystical experiences of the divine. But as we ascend into the highest heavens, we know we will face the temptations of the Evil One. We too may have those who will trick us with the delights of this world which lead us into the depths of darkness and desolation. This desolation that Jacob endured, that we will endure, can only be conquered with the blessing of the Angel himself, Jesus Christ, the Son of God. Welcoming us into the Covenant, the Lord offers himself to us so we, purified by his presence, experience who we are supposed to be: divine. Purified first and then blessed by God, we inherit all that the Lord promises us in the covenant. We must never forget, wherever we go, God is there with us, especially in times of desolation. We abandon ourselves into his will, accept God's purification from our own adulteries and idolatries, and allow the Lord to lead us up the ladder into heaven.

Under the Lord's guidance, divine inspirations give meaning and purpose to our lives; in exposing our emptiness, the Lord speaks to us heart to heart. In the journey of theosis, we pray that we too spiritually sacrifice ourselves to the Lord so we may gain the needed purity to seek the Face of God.

These images of the ladder, the gate, and the Lord's abiding presence touch our core for we all want to climb this ladder and encounter the divine as did Jacob. Created, we long for these divine experiences in which we behold God Face to Face.

> Who shall ascend the hill of the Lord? And who shall stand in his holy place? He who has clean hands and a pure heart, who does not lift up his soul to what is false and does not swear deceitfully. He will receive blessing from the Lord and righteousness from the

God of his salvation. Such is the generation of those who seek him, who seek the face of the God of Jacob. (Ps 24:3–6)

St. Bernard of Clairvaux unveils the beatific vision at the top of Jacob's ladder as our destiny, uniting us with the divine essence. When we seek the Face of God, we seek the beatific vision. God upholds us by his left hand under our head (like Jacob's pillow of stone—the Rock of Christ) and with his right hand embraces us with the light of his countenance, His Face, which is the beatific vision at the top of the ladder. This mystic saint describes the beatific vision of the Father.

> His left hand is under my head and his right hand embraces me. His left hand is symbolic of his unsurpassable charity which made him lay down his life for his friends, while his right hand portrays the beatific vision which he promised them and the joy of his majestic presence. The vision of God which makes us resemble him, and its incalculable delight are rightly figured by the right as hand, as the Psalmist joyfully sings: "In your right hand are everlasting joys" (Ps 56:2). In the left hand is well placed that admirable, memorable, and always to be remembered love, because the bride reclines on it and rests until evil is past.[1]

NATHANIEL'S LADDER

We understand anew the interpretation of Jacob's Ladder in Nathaniel's reception of the revelation of Jesus as the Christ. In John 1, Nathaniel heard many discussing who is this man Jesus, pondering whether he is the Messiah, the Christ. Yet Nathanial hears that Jesus is from Nazareth and immediately responds, "Can anything good come from Nazareth?" (John 1:47).

What we see in Nathaniel is a necessary characteristic for those who wish to ascend to God the Father. As Bernard of Clairvaux says, this journey of theosis requires all human abilities, starting with a heightened rationality produced by our engagement with Sacred Scripture. When we engage in contemplation, theosis, our minds, hearts, and souls ought never be veiled so we can experience the Logos' eternal, unchangeable and spiritual wisdom. "When we live according to God our mind should be intent on his

---

1. Bernard, *Treatises II*, 105.

invisible things and thus progressively be formed to his eternity, truth, and charity."[2]

Nathaniel shows us that if we like him choose to ponder the Sacred Scriptures, reflect on the historical events with our rational faculties, and search them for divine revelations, Christ will find us sitting under the fig tree. We too seek theosis with our full human capabilities wholly engaging our minds, hearts, and souls. Our God-given rationality guides us on the journey.

Nathaniel, as all of us do, receives an invitation for discipleship. Philip comes to tell Nathaniel of the Christ, and Nathaniel, receiving the message, thinks and responds. We too hear Jesus' divine invitation, "Come and see" (John 1:39).

Nathaniel desires perfect understanding of who the Christ is. Jesus, encountering Nathaniel, proclaims his purity, "There, truly, is an Israelite in whom there is no guile" (John 1:47). Nathaniel taken aback questions this man, Jesus, standing in front of him, "How do you know me?" (John 1:48). In a similar fashion, Mary echoes this great question, "How will this be?" (Luke 1:34). St. Paul questions upon being thrown off his horse, "Who are you, Lord?" (Acts 9:5) all reveal the stunned encounter, "Who is this man?"

The profundity of encountering a man who acts like God raises another question. Out of the purity of his heart, Nathaniel amazed asks, "How do you know me?" (John 1:48). Jesus responds truthfully, "Before Philip came to call you, I saw you under the fig tree" (John 1:50). Nathaniel, now convinced, proclaims, "Rabbi, you are the Son of God, you are the King of Israel" (John 1:49).

A prophetic revelation happens when Jesus talks with Nathaniel, saying, "You will see heaven open and the angels of God ascending and descending over the Son of Man" (John 1:51). Recalling Jacob's dream, Jesus promises Nathaniel it will be fulfilled when the Son of Man is lifted up (John 3:14).

Amazement comes. Nathaniel infused with God's insights understands immediately the dream of Jacob and his ladder. Jacob's theophany becomes infused with revelation. Nathaniel like Jacob sees angels ascending and descending and the person talking to him is the Lord, the same Lord who spoke to Jacob. The allegory comes to fulfillment. The person in front of Nathaniel is both Son of Man and the Son of God, Who unveils for us all the mysteries which Nathaniel was contemplating.

2. Augustine, *Trinity*, 333.

Nathaniel's interior questions live in us all. Who am I? Why am I? What is my purpose? Jesus answers them all—even without words. Through theosis, a divine and supernatural voice speaks in our heart of the Divine Presence. We, as did Nathaniel, seek the face of God. Through the stages of our *Lectio*, we encounter the true face of God. Nathaniel understands for whom our heart seeks: "He who has seen me sees the Father" (John 14:9). We too will see Jesus if we contemplate under our fig tree.

Nathaniel's response, "Rabbi, you are the Son of God, you are the King of Israel" (John 1:49). Without guile his heart is pure, his hands are clean, so he sees as the Psalmist tells, "He will receive blessing from the Lord and righteousness from the God of his salvation. Such is the generation of those who seek him, who seek the face of the God of Jacob" (Ps 24:4–6).

Nathaniel's heart is pure, full of faith, and quick to believe, yet he needs a firm foundation—the Rock of Christ—so the doubts of discipleship will not overwhelm him. Docility creates purity and Jesus calls Nathaniel to teach him not like a horse but as one whose eyes focus on the Lord.

> I will instruct you and teach you in the way you should go; I will counsel you with my eye upon you. Be not like a horse or a mule, without understanding, which must be curbed with bit and bridle, or it will not stay near you. (Ps 32:8–9)

Recognizing Christ as the Face of the Father displays the allegorical sense, so too this psalm unveils the tropological, or moral sense. We enter the goodness of Christ through discipleship. We do not limit and choose what we want to believe. Christ teaches us.

Jesus confronts Nathaniel, "You believe that I am the King of Israel just because I said: I saw you under the fig tree" (John 1:50). Jesus, recognizing Nathaniel's openness to transcendence, elevates him beyond the allegorical reality and reveals, I am the Divine Messiah. He also takes Nathanial beyond the tropological sense and reveals, I am the new Moses, the Rabbi who completes the law: the law of self-donation. Jesus promises Nathanial, "You will see greater things than these" (John 1:50). What could be greater than the revelation that Jesus is the King of Israel, the new Moses? The greatest revelation beholds and communes with the Face of God. This is the anagogical sense. To enter full *communio*—to partake in the divine nature and relate not as a disciple but as a son or daughter (2 Pet 1:3–4). The majesty and magnitude of this revelation completes Jacob's dream.

Through the synthesis of Aquinas' four-fold scriptural interpretation connecting with Jacob's ladder with Jesus' incarnation and his invitation to "Come and see," the scriptures reveal the detailed path of theosis. The ultimate essence of our human life journeys toward union with God: our nuptial marriage with the divine.

St. Bernard of Clairvaux recognizes and expresses this union, while Aquinas' scriptural interpretations mold this great wisdom into a paradigm so we can interpret all Sacred Scripture and recognize our calling: "Come and see." Jesus Christ, one of the divine persons of the Trinity, humbles himself in descent on the ladder into our world, fully human and divine, announcing himself as the Rock of Israel, the healing Oil of salvation, the Gate leading to the face of God the Father, and the One upon whom legions of Angels ascend and descend. The cross of Jesus Christ, the ladder, con- nects our world with the transcendent realms of heaven, where God the Father watches for our ascent to him. Jesus Christ in his baptism lowers himself into the chaotic waters seen in Genesis only to have the breath of God, the Spiritual Dove break through the heavens and open the path to a new creation. Now God the Father is well pleased for the completion of his mission is his crucifixion which tore open the temple veil to full com- munion with God the Father.

As St. John Paul II proclaimed, our faith is the window through which we see the divine essence, the ultimate blessing of human life, the Beatific Vision of God. In theosis, God welcomes us to live again fully in the Cov- enant of the Lord.

In brief, Jacob's ladder showed the form and the way to heaven. This dream provides a foundation to train our spiritual eyes to recognize the divinity and humanity of Jesus Christ. The ladder of the cross fulfills Jacob's hope and our hope for union and destiny with God.

THE FULL MEANING OF JESUS AND THE LADDER

As the Church Fathers and early Christians applied typology to Jacob, so we too read the Genesis accounts of his life in the same way. After Jesus' resur- rection, the early Christians, searching scriptures, understood Jesus Christ as the Son of God. God seeks us as he sought Jacob and Nathaniel to fulfill us. Indeed, the ladder of Jacob's dream provides a crucial interpretation of the cross revealing to us the intensity of God's love.

First, when Jesus was baptized, we see the beginning stages of fulfill- ment of Jacob's vision seeing the Lord God standing above the ladder. At Jesus' baptism, he saw the "heavens torn apart" and the Spirit came forth in the symbol of the dove and a voice proclaimed, "You are my beloved Son; with you I am well pleased" (Mark 1:11). Who then was Jesus Christ? He was the One standing at the top of Jacob's ladder, ready to descend and be become one with human beings in the restoration of the Covenant.

Secondly, a spiritual meaning emerges with the connection between Jesus' final Passover meal and God's promise to Jacob, "Behold, I am with you and will keep you wherever you go, and will bring you back to this land. For I will not leave you until I have done what I have promised you" (Gen 28:15). This foreshadows Jesus' promise given on the Passover, the night when he would tear open the heavens. "You did not choose me, but I chose you and appointed you that you should go and bear fruit and that your fruit should abide" (John 15:16). At the Passover, Jesus completes and fulfills the promise made to Jacob. "I will not leave you as orphans; I will come to you" (John 14:18).

Thirdly, we understand Jesus' sacrifice through the patriarch Isaac's willingness to be sacrificed. The journey to sacrifice Isaac allegorically prefigures Jesus because Isaac willingly obeys his father, Abraham, as he submits to the will of God. "Take your son, your only son Isaac, whom you love, and go to the land of Moriah, and offer him there as a burnt offering on one of the mountains of which I shall tell you" (Gen 22:2). For three days they journeyed up Mount Moriah, the place where the Jerusalem Temple was to be built, and Isaac fully participated yet God finally stopped this possible sacrifice. Jesus Christ later is truly sacrificed as the Son of God.

Fourth, Jesus is allegorically prefigured in the Rock upon which Jacob slept. Jacob takes the Rock anointing it with oil and proclaims a new name for this place, Bethel, which means "gate of heaven" or God's true home. Connections have been made between this Rock with the Rock at Massah and Meribah (Exod 17:6; Num 20:8). The Rock, the true presence of God allegorically, is Christ, Who pours forth living water. The image of this Rock, interpreted by Paul, "followed them, and the Rock was Christ" (1 Cor 10:3).

Fifth, many have recognized the parallels between the ladder and the cross, the symbol of sacrificial connection between heaven and earth. When Jesus died in the crucifixion, we see the fulfillment of Jesus' prophecy to Nathaniel. "You will see heaven open and the angels of God ascending and descending over the Son of Man" (John 1:51). Matthew 27:51–54 tells us of the veil being torn in two and those asleep raised. Was this the work of those angels that Jesus revealed to Nathaniel and Jacob?

> Behold, the curtain of the temple was torn in two, from top to
> bottom. And the earth shook, and the rocks were split. The tombs
> also were opened. And many bodies of the saints who had fallen
> asleep were raised, and coming out of the tombs after his resur-
> rection they went into the holy city and appeared to many. (Matt
> 27:51–53)

The tearing of the temple curtain veil symbolizes the new opening
to God the Father for his people. This reveals the end of Old Testament
sacrifices meant to purify the people of their sins. Instead, now the blood
of Christ perfectly purifies his people and the veil separating us from God
making him inaccessible to seekers wanting to climb the ladder, is torn—
ripped—from top to bottom.

> For if the blood of goats and bulls, and the sprinkling of defiled
> persons with the ashes of a heifer, sanctify for the purification of
> the flesh, how much more will the blood of Christ, who through
> the eternal Spirit offered himself without blemish to God, purify
> our conscience from dead works to serve the living God. (Heb
> 9:13–14)

Now we understand the Psalmist's plea that the gate at the top of the
ladder be opened.

> Open to me the gates of righteousness, that I may enter through
> them and give thanks to the Lord. This is the gate of the Lord;
> the righteous shall enter through it. I thank you that you have
> answered me and have become my salvation. The stone that the
> builders rejected has become the cornerstone. This is the Lord's
> doing; it is marvelous in our eyes. This is the day that the Lord has
> made; let us rejoice and be glad in it. (Ps 118:19–24)

The word used for the tearing open of heaven at Jesus' baptism and the
tearing of the temple veil is the same. God fulfills his promise to Jacob and
to all his descendants that God appears to us as he did in the dream and
speaks no longer behind veils but directly to us through his Divine Son, the
one promised to Abraham, Isaac, and Jacob.

Finally, an analogy exists between the Promised Land and Heavenly
Jerusalem. The place the Lord prepares for us is the heavenly Jerusalem.

> After this I looked, and behold, a door standing open in heaven!
> And the first voice, which I had heard speaking to me like a trum-
> pet, said, "Come up here, and I will show you what must take place
> after this." (Rev 4:1)

To understand the vision of Jacob, we immerse ourselves in Jacob's dream, to find fulfillment when the gate of the heavenly Jerusalem is opened, and we behold our God as his beloved.

> Then I saw a new heaven and a new earth, for the first heaven and the first earth had passed away, and the sea was no more. And I saw the holy city, new Jerusalem, coming down out of heaven from God, prepared as a bride adorned for her husband. And I heard a loud voice from the throne saying, "Behold, the dwelling place of God is with man. He will dwell with them, and they will be his people, and God himself will be with them as their God." (Rev 21:1-3)

In a commentary on Jacob's Ladder, St. Cesarius of Arles (+543), articulates the full spiritual meaning of Jacob's ladder interpreted in light of the Incarnation.

> Isaac, who sends forth his son, represents God the Father. Jacob, who is sent, designates the Christ our Teacher. The stone which he places under his head and which he anoints with oil, signifies the Savior. The ladder which reaches to the heavens is the figure of the Cross. The Lord supported on the ladder is Christ on the Cross.[3]

Interpreting the cross in light of Jacob's ladder shows the true way to the transcendent realm of God the Father. Christ comes down from heaven to be lifted up on the cross, connecting heaven and earth, unveiling his unconditional love—the gift-love of the Gospel through his sacrificial death. Annihilated in body, Jesus ascends to the heavens from where he came revealing his divine nature and consecrating his humanity as well as ours. Jacob's vision, Nathanial's experience, and our personal reflection through *Lectio Divina* completes this prophesized plan of salvation that started with a dream.

These images of the ladder with the gate that opens the transcendent realities of truth, goodness, and beauty, and Lord's abiding—loving—presence touch our core as human persons for we all want to climb and transcend this ladder and encounter the divine as did Jacob. Created by the Divine Artisan, we long for these divine experiences in which we behold God Face to Face. Pope Paul VI describes this.

> We must say it, almost trembling and praying, because it is his mystery, and his life, you know it: the Spirit, the Holy Spirit,

---

3. Cesarius, "Sermon 87," quoted in Pocetto, "The Image of Jacob's Ladder," 2.

animator and sanctifier of the Church, his divine breath, the wind of his sails, his unifying principle, his interior source of light and strength, his support and consoler, his source of charisms and songs, his peace and joy, his pledge and prelude of blessed and eternal life (Cfr. *Lumen Gentium*, 5).[4]

Entering theosis, we too walk with God hand in hand, comfortably without fear or trembling, but in perfect harmony because we are created to live in communion with the Trinity. The Holy Spirit infuses his life into us, sanctifying, and animating us, as Moses prays, blessing Aaron, blessing us all.

The Lord bless you and keep you; the Lord make his face to shine upon you and be gracious to you; the Lord lift up his countenance upon you and give you peace. (Num 6:24–26)

4. Paul VI, *Holy Spirit Animator.*

SECTION TWO

The Steps of Theosis

Chapter Four

THE FIRST STEP
The Beauty of Creation and Covenant

THE IDEAL OF DIVINE love perfects us. It is the only ideal worth living for. Every other ideal political, social, environmental, moral, and scientific creates false ideals. Love by its very nature acts, seeking and then revealing the goodness, truth, and beauty of the other. This memory rooted deeply in our minds recalls what once was. Eden: a place of perfect integrity, harmony, and clarity or radiance.

Our journey to the Beatific Vision begins in this recollection of the perfect enjoyment of God's presence in Eden. Theosis restores us on the path to once again partake and live with God in the glories of paradise, beholding the Face of God. Adam and Eve were immersed in this *communio*, a face-to-face embrace. In God's way of theosis, we are prepared to enjoy his heavenly visitation and intimacy within our soul. In the Garden of Eden, Adam and Eve lived in the delights of the Beatific Vision. Enjoying perfect communion with God the Father, they walked together in the cool of the evening. This situation of grace and light comes directly from God, as St. John of the Cross explains:

> How gently and lovingly you wake in my heart where in secret you dwell alone; and in your sweet breathing filled with good and glory, how tenderly you swell my heart with love.[1]

---

1. John of the Cross, *Poems*, 80.

God created us good and placed us in a beautiful universe. The truth that we belong to God in a beautiful communion remains in our soul, spiritually calling to us. We experience this participation when we have ears to listen and eyes to see.

In this harmony, the Spirit hovered over Adam and Eve, fulfilling and keeping them in the *communio*. The "labor" of the day was done, and they returned to *communio* with each other and with God. What awareness and ease they had being in love with one another and with God walking and dancing harmoniously through the simplicities of the garden, a temple of pure love.

Adam and Eve in all their splendor and majesty radiate the divine light for God clothed them personally with his own glory (Ps 34). Like the morning sun rising, the power, presence, and awe fill the horizons of our souls, burning away every mist and cloud until we see Beauty alone. This light displays the pure power of God as these two perfect creations reflect his divine loveliness in human form. Adam and Eve, Man and Woman, were made of God's goodness only to reflect and radiate God's beauty. One with each other, bone of my bone, flesh of my flesh; yet their beauty, power, and glory comes from God as they dwell with him perfectly. Adam and Eve enjoyed a perfect communion with God, entranced by his Holy Face.

St. John Paul II writes that we still sense this pathos and beauty when God "at the dawn of creation looked" upon the universe saying, "It is good."[2] We still have a profound interior hunger for that created perfection: the *communio personarum* we knew with God in the Garden of Eden.

God infuses himself as the Divine Artisan into every aspect of creation. From the smallest particles, inanimate and animate, to the largest of bodies, living or not, God infuses divine beauty in every corner of creation. "Through the work of creation the interior glory of God, which springs from the very mystery of the Divinity, is in a certain sense transferred "outside": into the creatures of the visible and invisible world, in proportion to their degree of perfection."[3] Divine beauty puts us on the journey to understanding God as Creator, as our Father, calling us into God's presence.

We see through his creative goodness that our entire life participates in God's uncreated beauty, as our interior life increasingly senses God's animating power within the depths of creation. Pope Benedict XVI interprets the complex thought of Divine Beauty.

2. John Paul II, *Artists*, sec. 1.

3. John Paul II, "General Audience, March 12, 1986."

Beauty itself cannot be reduced to simple pleasure of the senses: this would be to deprive it of its universality, its supreme value, which is transcendent. Perception requires an education, for beauty is only authentic in its link to the truth—of what would brilliance be, if not truth?—and it is at the same time 'the visible expression of the good, just as the good is the metaphysical expression of beauty.'"[4] [5]

At the conclusion of each day of creation, God saw that it was good. He saw it beautiful for beauty is goodness itself and goodness is beauty and both beauty and goodness reveal the Truth of God. We image his goodness, truth, and beauty which Aquinas calls transcendentals. These are objective properties, not contingent upon our subjective interpretation. We are objectively good and beautiful revealing the truth of who we are. The creation narrative reveals the divine harmony of these transcendentals, first in God's Uncreated *Communio Personarum*, then in our created *communio personarum* with God.

Because God reveals his power, glory, and majesty in the splendor and beauty of creation. St. John Paul II challenges and even implores artists, to reveal and listen for that first, divine creative explosion of goodness, beauty, and truth described in Genesis. He writes,

> None can sense more deeply than you artists, ingenious creators
> of beauty that you are, something of the pathos with which God at
> the dawn of creation looked upon the work of his hands.[6]

Understanding this divine pathos of beauty, living in this mystery, more of the face of God appears to us as Father, the great Creator of all that is. "Such is the generation of those who seek him, who seek the face of the God of Jacob" (Ps 24:6).

The Genesis Narrative discloses the creative power of God's unconditional love inviting us into a covenantal relationship with him. To understand our relationship with God, we learn to love each other freely, faithfully, and totally as God does with us. This is shalom. When we live in shalom—harmony and unity—with the Trinity, we belong to divine *Communio Personarum*. Dwelling in shalom with other people, we reflect this communion. The essence of communion dwells in a covenantal

---

4. John Paul II, *Artists*, sec. 3.

5. Benedict XVI, *Via Pulchritudinis*, II.1.

6. John Paul II, *Artists*, sec. 1.

relationship, a mutual exchange of body, heart, mind, and will: total gift-love. Gift love is nuptial union. It completes us as God himself wishes to complete us. The whole of creation displays this unity and harmony: God the Father, God the Son, and God the Holy Spirit, dwelling in our heart, mind, and soul so we partake, share, and live in his essence.

COMMUNIO PERSONARUM: THE UNION OF MALE AND FEMALE

St. John Paul II interprets the Genesis narratives in light of God's passion to unite with us. He analyzed the characteristics of the *imago dei* as transcendence, subjectivity, self-determination, and an opening to others. He also emphasized the necessity of union between male and female for the fullness of being in the *imago dei*. His *Theology of the Body* restores the memory of the Garden of Eden in which man, woman, and God all dwelt in perfect harmony.

St. John Paul II used his Wednesday audiences to explore this new insight of the harmony of man and woman in union with their Creator. *The Theology of the Body* explores this human and divine intimacy. The teachings of this theology become the pathway to the divine: the Uncreated *Communio Personarum*. We understand the Uncreated *Communio Personarum*, the Holy Trinity, through the created *communio personarum*, nuptial unity as experienced by Adam and Eve. In them he stated that male and female complement each other, creating the possibility for intimacy. This is the created *communio personarum* that reveals God.

The unified scriptural message reveals God's unwavering desire to abide with us. We are his ultimate creative act, and he seeks to envelop us into his presence. To do this, God covenants himself with us. He chooses to exchange his total self, humbling himself and incarnating and even dying on the cross, inviting us to receive his gift and exchange our total self so we can be enveloped by his presence.

This is the Mystery of covenantal theology. One chooses to exchange oneself for the other unconditionally. In the Trinity, the Father exchanges himself—gifts himself completely—to the Son and the Son exchanges himself completely; and through this exchange, the Spirit of Love exists binding all three into a *Communio Personarum*. Adam and Eve created in the image and likeness of God exchange themselves to each other creating a *communio*—a relationship of unconditional and pure love.

To expound on gift-love, the *communio personarum*, St. John Paul II explains the differences between the two creation accounts in Genesis. In the first creation account, Genesis 1:1–27, St. John Paul II describes the human powers that identify man as male and female both being made in the image of God.

> In the first chapter, the narrative of the creation of man affirms directly, right from the beginning, that man was created in the image of God as male and female. The narrative of the second chapter, on the other hand, does not speak of the "image of God." But in its own way it reveals that the complete and definitive creation of "man" (subjected first to the experience of original solitude) is expressed in giving life to that *communio personarum* that man and woman form. In this way, the Yahwist narrative agrees with the content of the first narrative.[7]

This *imago dei* gifts us with transcendence, subjectivity, self-determination, and an openness to others. These four become the essence of this new theology. They are the powers that make us share the divine image and likeness. Through these four shared characteristics, Adam and Eve know and experience divine love for they have free will: to choose to live in communio with each other and God or not.

The first narrative establishes our image as being created in God's image. Adam has the power of transcendence. He has a human nature and rationality. Because of this transcendency which differentiated him from the animals and the rest of creation, his mind, heart, and soul could ponder creation and even understand its complexities, unlike the animals. His mind was illuminated. His will was balanced. His mind and will worked harmoniously together. He experienced the great truth, goodness, and beauty of the universe and his transcendency allowed him to claim dominion over the animals.

Mostly, however, as the second narrative explains, Adam communed with God for there was no one like him. Adam, created with personal awareness, transcended all of creation but was alone. In the second account Eve is created from the side of Adam. God puts a deep sleep upon Adam only to rise and behold the face of Eve. This beholding reveals Adam's innate desire to be one with another human person: to be in communio with another who fulfills and completes his solitude.

---

7. John Paul II, *Communion of Persons.*

> As we have already seen, in his original solitude man acquires a
> personal consciousness in the process of distinction from all liv-
> ing beings (animalia). At the same time, in this solitude, he opens
> up to a being akin to himself, defined in Genesis (2:18, 20) as "a
> helper fit for him." This opening is no less decisive for the person
> of man; in fact, it is perhaps even more decisive than the distinc-
> tion itself.[8]

Created with subjectivity, we determine ourselves. In reality, we are a
universe unto ourselves with these four John Paulian qualities. This is the
power of free-will. But we only perfect ourselves if through our subjectivity
we open ourselves—open our ability to love—to another person.

Adam comprehensively sees creation and the glories of the animals
and the beauty of the universe, yet he saw no one like himself. He knows he
is alone, and God is so unlike him. More importantly, alone he knows he is
not God and cannot create another self.

In his experience of solitude, Adam was incomplete. Without another,
he knows, we know, we need friends. This transcendent understanding: we
were made for relationship, making us similar to God. Our bodies hunger
for another body to touch, feel, and unite. Our minds seek to know, that
is to understand the other as a who, one who challenges and sharpens my
own thoughts and understanding. Our hearts yearn for connection, a deep,
personal, spiritual soul to soul bond in which two hearts become one. God
is a Triune Relationship: Father, Son, and Holy Spirit. All three relate with
one another substantially. Adam related to no one substantially. He did not
have another self, that is a friend.

Understanding the concept of a friendship, Adam was a person with
a heart and mind that gave him personhood—the capability to befriend
another—he experienced an "opening and expectation of a 'communion of
persons.'"[9] Created with God's plan for a communion of persons planted
within his soul, Adam sought a someone like himself. This opening asked
for a consubstantial relationship with a someone who was a "helper fit for
him" (Gen 2:18–20). God created Eve for him because it is not good for
Adam to be alone. Adam exclaims when he beholds his other self, "Bone
of my bone, flesh of my flesh!" Adam rejoices in one who is like him so he
could exchange himself with her and she could gift herself to him and they
become like God, a triune relationship: man, woman and the bond between

8. John Paul II, *Communion of Persons.*

9. John Paul II, *Communion of Persons.*

48

them: love. Or as St. John Paul says, "Through the same words of Genesis 2:23, they indicate the new consciousness of the sense of one's own body. It can be said that this sense consists in a mutual enrichment."[10] Together they knew they were made in the image of God to gift themselves to each other as does the Father, Son, and Holy Spirit.

Hence, the second creation narrative concerning Eve being made from the rib of Adam completes the content of the first narrative. Humanity includes fertility because humanity is male and female, different but complementary. In this first creation narrative, St. John Paul II explains why we have bodies and what our bodies do: unite and procreate. He writes,

> In the mystery of creation—on the basis of the original and constituent "solitude" of his being—man was endowed with a deep unity between what is, humanly and through the body, male in him and what is, equally humanly and through the body, female in him. On all this, right from the beginning, the blessing of fertility descended, linked with human procreation (cf. *Gn* 1:28).[11]

Sharing our bodies encompasses the whole of friendship. It is not just a physical or even sexual experience. It is a total expression of self in which two people whether bonded in marriage or bonded through friendship share our complete self. Sharing the complete self fulfills and perfects the four John Paulian characteristics. We are self-determining subjects not only open to gift love, but also willingly give ourselves. In this self-donation we find the ultimate meaning of sharing our bodies: transcendency.

A community of persons shares life and love, and no greater love exists than the love between friends, especially man and woman laying down their lives for each other. This creates the family where two or more persons willingly determine that the other in light of Divine Love is more important than the self. Nevertheless, to grow in love, to draw closer to God, and to desire *communio*, we must experience that first solitude as St. John Paul II expresses this.

> In this way the meaning of man's original unity, through masculinity and femininity, is expressed as an overcoming of the frontier of solitude. At the same time, it is an affirmation—with regard to both human beings—of everything that constitutes man in solitude.[12]

10. John Paul II, *Communion of Persons*.

11. John Paul II, *Communion of Persons*.

12. John Paul II, *Communion of Persons*.

St. John Paul II calls the relationship between male and female, a special reciprocity.

> Furthermore, the communion of persons could be formed only on the basis of a "double solitude" of man and of woman, that is, as their meeting in their distinction from the world of living beings (*animalia*), which gave them both the possibility of being and existing in a special reciprocity.[13]

We image the Trinity in our very being, a place of community and unity, a place to belong and bond where our soul dwells in a family not only with another human being but also with the Father, Son, and Holy Spirit. St. John Paul II expresses his concern about the term "community" saying,

> The term "community" could also be used here, if it were not generic and did not have so many meanings. *Communio* expresses more, with greater precision, since it indicates precisely that "help" which is derived, in a sense, from the very fact of existing as a person "beside" a person. In the Bible narrative this fact becomes *eo ipso* - in itself - the existence of the person "for" the person, since man in his original solitude was, in a way, already in this relationship. That is confirmed, in a negative sense, precisely by this solitude.[14]

John Paul says that we are the image of God in the union of male and female. He writes the following.

> The function of the image is to reflect the one who is the model, to reproduce its own prototype. Man becomes the image of God not so much in the moment of solitude as in the moment of communion. Right "from the beginning," he is not only an image in which the solitude of a person who rules the world is reflected, but also, and essentially, an image of an inscrutable divine communion of persons.[15]

Communio includes friendship, finding another self, as well as finding oneself in friendship with God directly. Jesus discussing marriage with his disciples reveals another type of relationship: those who choose to isolate themselves for the sake of the kingdom (Matt 19:12). This teaching, voluntary celibacy in imitation of Jesus himself, opens a person to the

13. John Paul II, *Communion of Persons*.

14. John Paul II, *Communion of Persons*.

15. John Paul II, *Communion of Persons*.

divine directly for they become friends of God directly without intermediary. Some persons experience the call to direct relationship with God as revealed in the many monasteries, convents, and sanctuaries throughout history. St. John Paul II describes our desire to please God in this way.

> "To please the Lord" has love as its foundation. This foundation arises from a further comparison. The unmarried person is anxious about how to please God, while the married man is anxious also about how to please his wife. In a certain sense, the spousal character of "continence for the sake of the kingdom of God" is apparent here. Man always tries to please the person he loves. Therefore, "to please God" is not without this character that distinguishes the interpersonal relationship between spouses. On the one hand, it is an effort of the man who is inclined toward God and seeks the way to please him, that is, to actively express his love. On the other hand, an approval by God corresponds to this aspiration. By accepting man's efforts, God crowns his own work by giving a new grace. Right from the beginning, this aspiration has been his gift. "Being anxious how to please God" is therefore a contribution of man in the continual dialogue of salvation that God has begun.[16]

Charity is the heart of love. Love aspires to please the other. Those who by a unique grace anxiously desire to please God alone through celibacy inspires all of humanity to see the power and depth of Divine Love for Love as we know conquers all and drives out all fears. Out of all the graces and gifts given by God, love is the only one that remains.

St. John Paul II quotes St. John of the Cross about the role of love.

> Therefore God communicates himself most to that soul that has progressed farthest in love, which means that its will is more in conformity with the will of God. And the soul that has attained complete conformity and likeness of will is completely united and transformed in God supernaturally.[17]

Mystical contemplation leads us up the ladder to find Divine Love. This theophany Jacob experienced outlines for us all our quest for divine wisdom rather than human. Created male and female, we cry out for union, a friendship that satisfies our desire for love. Growing, shaping, and

---

16. John Paul II, *Redemption of the Body*, 215.

17. John Paul II, *Faith*, 50, quoting John of the Cross, *Ascent*, II.5.4.

climbing the ladder of theosis, St. John of the Cross reveals the point of our quest: heavenly treasures.

> Just as men mount by means of ladders and climb up to posses-
> sions and treasures and thing that are in strong places, even so
> also, by means of this secret contemplation without knowing how,
> the soul ascends and climbs up to a knowledge and possession of
> the good things and treasures of heaven.[18]

For those grounded in earthly realities, the ladder becomes the way to transcend. Yet transcendency must be a choice. Why chose this path? No matter how we live, married, single, or celibate, the ladder comes down from heaven calling us to climb up to the transcendent treasures that perfectly complete and fulfill our heart. St. John of the Cross interprets Jacob's ascent.

> For this ladder of contemplation, which, as we have said, comes
> down from God, is prefigured by that ladder which Jacob saw as
> he slept, whereon angels were ascending and descending, from
> God to man, and from man to God, Who Himself was leaning
> upon the end of the ladder. All this, says Divine Scripture, took
> place by night, when Jacob slept, in order to express how secret is
> this road and ascent to God, and how different from that of man's
> knowledge. This is very evident, since ordinarily that which is of
> the greatest profit in it—namely, to be ever losing oneself and be-
> coming as nothing—is considered the worst thing possible; and
> that which is of least worth, which is for a soul to find consolation
> and sweetness (wherein it ordinarily loses rather than gains), is
> considered best.[19]

The inscrutable *Communio Personarum* of the Trinity calls us to climb for it awakens in us our desire to adore.

Awakening our heart through theosis also awakens the inscrutable community of persons within us, creating ecstatic worship and adoration. In this ecstasy of finding *communio*, we are no longer incomplete, longing for the face and voice of our beloved because we are made for communio both created and uncreated, fulfilled perfectly with divine love, as the Song of Solomon invokes,

> Arise, my love, my beautiful one, and come away. O my dove, in
> the clefts of the rock, in the crannies of the cliff, let me see your

18. John of the Cross, *Dark Night*, 164.

19. John of the Cross, *Dark Night*, 164.

face, let me hear your voice, for your voice is sweet, and your face
is lovely. (Song 2:13–14)

PERSONAL REFLECTION: MY OWN LADDER

It was Sunday. I sat on the bench. To the east lay the river and to the west
the hill. I was in the middle. The street was empty. In a few hours the tour-
ists would be bustling about, and the cafés would be steaming their famous
Italian cappuccinos. Yet for the moment, it was quiet, a place to pray. The
sun was just coming up and the rays started to illumine the hill. It was not
any hill, but the second most famous hill, the first being Golgotha.

Centuries ago, the place where I sat was a swamp, and the trail, now
street, led to the hill, a place of Roman execution, Vatican Hill, one of the
seven hills of Rome. As I sat, I looked up at the hill. Now instead of a place
horror and torture, it was the place of worship.

The Basilica glowed in the morning sun, as the sun rose on this Trinity Sunday. I looked up and the cross on top of the cupola gleamed. That

cross marked the spot where the Romans executed the person for whom the basilica is named: St. Peter.

A few miles from the Hill stands a church, Quo Vadis. In the Gospel, Jesus tells St. Peter leave any town and shake the dust off your feet if they did not accept you. St. Peter being hunted down as a Christian left Rome as they sought to crucify him for they rejected his God for their gods. As he was leaving, he encountered the risen Lord, and Peter asked, "Quo vadis? Where are you going?" Jesus replied, "Roman eo iterum crucifigi! I am going to Rome to be crucified again." This time St. Peter followed and got behind Jesus not in front of him.

On Vatican Hill, St. Peter was crucified upside down on a cross for he felt unworthy to imitate his Savior who was hung upside right on that most famous hill, Golgotha.

The obelisk, a spear shaped monument made of pink granite that is eighty-four feet tall and stands in the middle of St. Peter's Square. An artifact from Egypt brought over to Rome by the Roman Emperor Caligula in 37 BC reminds the world of the power of Roman Empire which conquered from England to Jerusalem. But now it reminds the world that every great kingdom from the Egyptians to the Romans to the National Socialist German Workers Party (Nazi), and even to the Nationalist Fascist Party (PNF) commonly called Fascism all fail, all fall except the kingdom of God. The cross of St. Peter still stands two thousand years later.

That day, I would walk up that Via, just as St. Peter ages ago walked, him to his crucifixion; my walk was to my ordination.

That day, I would walk up the path, the Via della Conciliazione and in a few hours the successor to St. Peter, St. John Paul II would place his hands on me and declare: Tu es sacerdos in aeternum secundum ordinem Melchisedech. You are a priest forever in the order of Melchizedek (Ps 110).

As I looked at the hill, where Michelangelo's famous Cupola rises almost four hundred feet, supported by four pillars. One pillar is dedicated to St. Helena, the mother of Constantine who legalized Christianity in 313 AD. The second pillar dedicated to St. Longinus the Roman Centurion who lanced Jesus with his spear and tradition holds he converted by the Blood of the Cross. The third pillar dedicated to St. Andrew, St. Peter's brother, holds up another column, a prominent position, as both brothers gave their lives for the Lord: St. Peter upside down on the cross and St. Andrew on a cross in the shape of an X. The fourth pillar is dedicated to St. Veronica, who wipes Jesus' face on his way to the crucifixion, making the true icon of the face of Jesus. In the center of this cupola is the altar determined by the recent archaeological digs to be the exact spot of St. Peter's crucifixion 2000 years earlier. It was the spot where I would kneel and St. John Paul II would place his hands upon my head and I would be expected to become part of the litany of the saints, the song sung before any priestly ordination. I too would become a pillar—more like a fence post—of the church

As I sat, I prayed. I sought wisdom, asking is this wise to walk with Peter, with Jesus to this place of crucifixion, or should I too shake the dust off my shoes and walk my way? St. Paul, another martyr, spoke:

> I have been crucified with Christ. It is no longer I who live, but Christ who lives in me. And the life I now live in the flesh I live by faith in the Son of God, who loved me and gave himself for me. (Gal 2:20)

In the Old and New Testaments, the priest was ordained for two reasons. First, the priest was ordained to pray for himself and for his people. The second, the priest offered sacrifice to the Lord on behalf of his sins and the sins of the people. During the baptismal ritual, the priest pours water over the person and then anoints the person with the Oil of Christ, Chrism Oil, with these words, "I anoint you priest, prophet and king."

Today, already anointed in the common priesthood of the baptized, I would be anointed in that same oil and marked permanently anew, not as a common priest, but as ministerial priest: the one who lays down his life for his sheep as did Jesus, as did St. Peter, as did St. John Paul II. On that spot where the blood of St. Peter poured out, so too it is expected that my blood—my life—will be poured out. So, I prayed with Solomon asking for living wisdom:

> God of my ancestors, Lord of mercy, you who have made all things by your word And in your wisdom have established humankind to rule the creatures produced by you, And to govern the world in holiness and righteousness, and to render judgment in integrity of heart:
>
> Give me Wisdom, the consort at your throne, and do not reject me from among your children; For I am your servant, the child of your maidservant, a man weak and short-lived and lacking in comprehension of judgment and of laws. Indeed, though one be perfect among mortals, if Wisdom, who comes from you, be lacking, that one will count for nothing. You have chosen me king over your people and magistrate over your sons and daughters.

You have bid me build a temple on your holy mountain and an altar in the city that is your dwelling place, a copy of the holy tabernacle which you had established from of old. Now with you is Wisdom, who knows your works and was present when you made the world; Who understands what is pleasing in your eyes and what is conformable with your commands.

Send her forth from your holy heavens and from your glorious throne dispatch her That she may be with me and work with me, that I may know what is pleasing to you. For she knows and understands all things, and will guide me prudently in my affairs and safeguard me by her glory;

Thus my deeds will be acceptable, and I will judge your people justly and be worthy of my father's throne.

For who knows God's counsel, or who can conceive what the Lord intends? For the deliberations of mortals are timid, and uncertain our plans. For the corruptible body burdens the soul and the earthly tent weighs down the mind with its many concerns.

Scarcely can we guess the things on earth, and only with difficulty grasp what is at hand; but things in heaven, who can search them out?

Or who can know your counsel, unless you give Wisdom and send your holy spirit from on high? Thus were the paths of those on earth made straight, and people learned what pleases you, and were saved by Wisdom. (Wis 9:1–18 NABRE)

After my prayer, I looked up, towards the loggia, the main portico on the second floor of St. Peter's where the new popes are announced. Ten years previous, a Polish Cardinal stood at that window and when he did, he himself went through his metanoia. He was no longer Karol Wojtyla, Cardinal of Krakow, but now a new man stood there, John Paul II, the first non-Italian pope in some five hundred years.

He spoke. I listened. "Be Not Afraid!" Those words that echoed down the Piazza into the Via della Conciliazione, I heard whispering in my ears, spoken as though they answered my prayer. I stood up and started walking towards those doors. The man who was about to ordain me had the keys to open those doors and lock them. Those doors open to heaven and the gates of hell will not prevail. Those are the same doors and the same key St. Peter received from the Master two thousand years previous. This indeed is a great mystery: a metanoia.

That same Master called St. Peter out of the boat into the raging waves and told him to walk. So too with St. John Paul II, he was called from a country afar to step into the world stage as the new key holder. I too was called to cross that threshold to walk by faith, not by sight. To walk with my eyes fixed on Christ as did St. Peter, as did St. John Paul II, as did St. John of the Cross and enter the Way of Nothing.

When St. Peter faltered, Jesus asked, "Why are you afraid?" St. John Paul II also struggled to walk by faith, but he learned from his meditation that we all must keep our eyes fixed on Christ. Now, I began my journey to walk on the water of faith and I too would learn to keep my eyes on Christ, especially when the turmoil of being a priest would pierce my heart.

St. Catherine, a woman clothed with profound mystical insights, confronted every fear in her life and counseled the greatest of sinners and saints in her time when the Catholic world was broiling in scandal, turmoil, and disease. This woman who spoke heart to heart with Jesus offers this advice when fear freezes us.

> Your chief desire ought to be to slay your selfish will so that it neither seeks nor wants anything but to follow my gentle Truth, Christ crucified, by seeking the honor and glory of my name and the salvation of souls.[20]

As I walked toward the Hill, I focused on the loggia crossing the white line into another country, Vatican City State. That famous white line became the wall of national security, a refuge for those Allied dissidents seeking escape from Nazi occupied Rome during World War II. I casually crossed it knowing that many were shot trying to cross it just decades ago. That white line is etched in every threshold of every Catholic Church designating the church a place of refuge for every sinner and saint. That same white line etched in the Krakow Cathedral saved the saint forty years previous who was about to ordain me.

Bernini's Columns invited, then embraced me welcoming me into the priesthood of the Catholic Church and I too would be written into her saintly history, though sadly disgraceful history at times too.

In a few hours, I would no longer be who I was, I would become an ambassador of Christ, his servant. Eight long years of study and prayer, four years of daily Eucharistic Adoration, reception of Holy Communion, Study of Latin, Greek, Italian, monthly counseling and confession, work, travel, and military training would culminate as St. John Paul II would impose his hands on my head and call down the Holy Spirit upon me.

---

20. Catherine of Siena, *Dialogue*, 179.

I, in turn, would promise absolute obedience to him and his successor. I would promise under pain of mortal sin to pray the Divine Office faithfully every day for the rest of my life, not only for my personal sanctity, but more importantly the sanctity of the Church. I promised to give my life completely and totally now and forever to the Bride of Christ his Church. I had to be faithful to her as a celibate priest in the good times and bad; sickness and health till death in this world and everlasting life in the heavenly kingdom marked as a priest forever in the line of Melchizedek.

This is metanoia and this metanoia changes the heart, for the heart is a gift made to be given away, daily. This is the *Communio Personarum* where the priest no longer lives for himself but lives for Christ; and as he offers himself up on his cross, he pours his life out so that the Holy Spirit will pour his divine life into the heart of the priest. This is the fulfillment of *Lectio Divina* in which reading the scriptures, Jesus is not another character, he is our companion on the journey walking with us, inviting us to follow as St. Peter followed Jesus back into Rome. This is agape love—sacrificial love—in which the priest befriends Christ and as his friend, the priest becomes another Christ: a suffering servant. This was the day, I would ask Quo vadis and Jesus would say, "Come and see" (John 1:39).

Chapter Five

THE SECOND STEP
Restoration and Reconciliation

How does our divine Creator draw us out of the Fall? To answer the question of restoration, we contemplate through *Lectio Divina* the tragedy of the Fall. In this second step of theosis, we confront evil by dwelling in the *Communio Personarum*, the sacred holiness of the Trinity.

Seeing all of creation as good, very good indeed, God loved all he created, most importantly God loved the crowning of his creation: Adam and Eve making a sacred covenant with them on the seventh day infusing his divine dignity within.

In the beginning, all of creation intermingled harmoniously, partaking freely of the Divine Presence. Both angelic spirits and human beings participated fully according to their ability in the Divine Dignity. Intertwined, God's Glory shined upon us all. Yet, in the spirit world, envy struck. Some angels rebelled declaring, *Non Serviam*: I will not serve! In these angels, God found wickedness (Job 4:18) because they were filled with covetousness. "By the envy of the Devil, death came into the world" (Wis 2:4). Because of this enmity and envy, a great battle ensued.

> Now war arose in heaven, Michael and his angels fighting against
> the dragon. And the dragon and his angels fought back, but he was
> defeated, and there was no longer any place for them in heaven.
> And the great dragon was thrown down, that ancient serpent, who
> is called the devil and Satan, the deceiver of the whole world—he

was thrown down to the earth, and his angels were thrown down with him. (Rev 12:7–9)

Some Old Testament prophets exposed the powers of the Evil One. Ezekiel sees Satan as an Accuser, an Adversary, and an object of Terror (Ezek 28:19). Isaiah proclaims allegorically Satan—the Day Star: the one who bears the light; becomes the one who brings forth darkness for he has fallen.

> How you are fallen from heaven, O Day Star, son of Dawn! How you are cut down to the ground, you who laid the nations low! You said in your heart, "I will ascend to heaven; above the stars of God I will set my throne on high; I will sit on the mount of assembly in the far reaches of the north; I will ascend above the heights of the clouds; I will make myself like the Most High." But you are brought down to Sheol, to the far reaches of the pit. (Isa 14:12–15)

Satan, a model of perfection, filled with wisdom, a living creature with outstretched wings praising God, fell. Created beauty himself, Satan glorified God through his brightness. Yet he became filled with guilt, sin, and violence because he along with all pure spirits and human beings have free will. Our Creator endows us with love and love must be free to choose either good or evil. Through the prophet, we understand God's accusation against Satan's choice, "Your heart has grown proud because of your beauty" (Ezek 28:17).

Adam and Eve worship God; yet Satan in his deception seeks to pervert their worship and reject the Creator of creation. Adam and Eve exposed to the demonic forces within the Garden, Satan cunningly infiltrates their thinking to control their wills.

In harmony with the Creator's will, the Evil One—the Serpent—comes seducing Eve, insinuating into her mind and heart the idea that she will rule and be like God if she disobeys the ancient prohibition from eating of this tree, the Tree of the Knowledge of Good and Evil. This tree offered comprehensive knowledge which only a God above all created beings could ever comprehend all the complexities of the universe.

The serpent induced Eve to look at the tree with its fruit not as something to fear and respect, but to indulge in and come to the secret and hidden knowledge that the Divine Architect did not want them to know just yet. Unprepared to understand this knowledge, that is to determine good and evil, they stole the knowledge prematurely in opposition to God's authority. They denied the law of self-donation, becoming irresponsible and immature.

The father of lies deceives and entices them with powers and authority that is not theirs. It belongs to the Creator. However, "When the woman saw that the tree was good for food, and that it was a delight to the eyes, and that the tree was to be desired to make one wise, she took of its fruit and ate, and she also gave some to her husband who was with her, and he ate" (Gen 3:6). This tragedy of eating was not merely eating something, but sharing a meal with their deceiver who seduced them, threatening them with the terror of his power and presence.

Eve communicates these cancerous thoughts to Adam, who listening and watching the temptation, believes them too. So, he took the fruit of the tree of comprehensive and universal knowledge and ate. With the Fall, their inner beauty and grandeur metamorphoses. They, we all, become possessed by the father of lies who constantly tricks us making his thoughts our own thoughts: we are greater than God. Our creator, Adam and Eve's creator, is the devil now, recreating them in his image: the Father of lies.

> You are of your father the devil, and your will is to do your father's desires. He was a murderer from the beginning, and does not stand in the truth, because there is no truth in him. When he lies, he speaks out of his own character, for he is a liar and the father of lies. (John 8:44)

Filled with shame, lost in a sea of lies, Adam and Eve no longer behold the face of God. Because of this, God lost full communion with humans who no longer have clean hands or a pure heart.

Thus the gate to the Garden was sealed and locked by the Seraphim Angels protecting Adam and Eve from eating of the Tree of Life in a state of death. Original Sin deprives us of his grace, that is the Face of God. Theosis through *Lectio Divina* restores our relationship with God, removing the very cause of our losing sanctifying grace teaching us, restoring us, to full communion

Deceived by the deceiver, Adam and Eve become divorced from their original identity. Examine how the Serpent entices Eve. Created as queen and mother of the Garden, here she bears eternal fruit freely and securely. In her Fall, she reduces herself into selfish solitude, using her other self, Adam, for her happiness. In using him, she brazenly lusts to satisfy her needs only.

Adam, the protector and priest of the Garden, watches this seduction take place abandoning his post to defend and keep the Garden and his spouse safe. He rejects his responsibility and now suffers intensely. Seduced, he divorces his wife and watches the Serpent entrap and entangle her. Now he toils and labors in vain for he no longer glorifies his Creator, nor respects his helpmate, but hides behind the fig leaf for protection.

Immediately following the Fall of his creative genius, God comes searching for his lost children, Adam and Eve, crying out: "Where are you, Adam? Where are you, Eve?" Hidden behind fig leaves they knew something drastically damaged their integrity: their goodness, truth, and beauty. They are not captains of creation; they are captured creations of Satan. Fallen, they divorce themselves from their Maker and lose his sanctifying grace.

Satan hopes we too do not recognize or acknowledge his spirit infiltrating our minds, memory, and hearts, seducing us to partake in those three temptations better known as hedonism, materialism, or scientism. Even more insidious, these temptations seem so casual and usual because they hide and deny the very existence of anything evil. These ideologies falsely promise choices without moral responsibility or eternal consequences. Satan twisted Adam and Eve's responsibility making them think that they would be more human without God. In reality they reduced themselves to his humanism, doubting and denying their divine dignity. They were the realized *imago dei*: humanity fully alive in God, but now reduced to beastly behaviors.

The temptations that befell Adam and Eve now become ours. Satan now attacks our *imago dei* and reduces us to seek solely the human pleasures, earthly possessions, and worldly powers. We know these as the flesh, the world, and the devil. He tempts us to become mere shadows focusing only on our earthly identity, denying our heavenly image.

Envious of our divinity and dignity—we participate in the essence of the Divine Presence—the Serpent, Satan communicates not with words, but malignant ideas seeping into our minds that makes us feel as if they are our own. The great deception occurs and continues to occur as the Serpent constantly instills ideas into our minds that make us feel equal if not greater than God. We too have comprehensive knowledge of creation. Do we?

In temptation these thoughts become desires and move subtly in our hearts and influence the direction of our interior life. Eve followed these ideas and took the fruit and ate of it. The serpent deceived Eve through envy and now the demon has the suggestive power over her and her body, mind, and heart.

Like Adam and Eve, our goodness and beauty become the source of our ugliness. This is the Fall from grace. Adam and Eve's sin still impacts our lives in our own experience of evil today and our own lingering sense of interior and exterior corruption. Because we remember this perfect *communio*, we seek restoration to that full communion with God, Father, Son, and Holy Spirit we once had. This second step of theosis delivers us from the shadows of evil introduced by the Fall.

ORIGINAL SIN

The Fall began what we call Original Sin, a sin communicated to all human beings. This great mystery of Original Sin causes our personal sin, the plague of human history. Sin, so cruel and corrosive, alienates us from God, our very selves, and from *communio*.

> The Credo of the People of God teaches that human nature after original sin is no longer in the "state at which it was at first in our first parents." It is "fallen" since it is deprived of sanctifying grace, and also of other gifts, which in the state of original justice constituted the perfection of this nature.[1]

St. John Paul II states his idea directly: Original Sin deprives us of sanctifying grace. Because of this definition, we are alienated from God the source of our clarity, integrity, and harmony. We lose our friendship with God.

Unlike the understanding of Original Sin as total depravity, St. John Paul II, in several talks in the Fall of 1986, explains a more mature and thoughtful interpretation. For centuries, the unofficial interpretation of Original Sin corrupted our understanding of what the human person is. Many believe we are totally depraved, infected with the incurable disease having been conceived in sin.

In truth, Original Sin is human weakness derived from our lack of sanctifying grace which coordinates our passions, drives, emotions, feelings into a wholeness. In sanctifying grace, we may behold God's face. Without this grace, our wholeness is broken. Left to our whims and desires

---

1. John Paul II, " General Audience, October 8, 1986."

of our concupiscence, we then abuse our freewill, the law of liberty (Jas 1–2; Gal 5–6).

> Sin as "disobedience" to the law is best manifested in its character of "disobedience" to personal God: to God as Legislator, who is at the same time a loving Father. This message, already expressed profoundly in the Old Testament (cf. *Hos* 11: 1–7), will find its fullest enunciation in the parable of the prodigal son (cf. *Lk* 15, 18–21). In any case, disobedience to God, that is, opposition to his creative and saving will, including man's desire "to achieve his end outside of God", is an "abuse of freedom" (*Gaudium et Spes*, 13).[2]

Original Sin becomes the spark of personal sin. This spark described as concupiscence or a more modern term, our addictiveness, becomes our shame. Yet, shame means total depravity—I am worthless. This is the mindset of many who falsely believe shame makes us unworthy of love. Shame is what Adam and Eve experienced, but God does not shame them. He comes looking to restore them. "Original sin must constantly be considered in reference to the mystery of the redemption carried out by Jesus Christ, the Son of God, who "for us men and for our salvation became man."[3]

To advance the Church in spiritual maturity, St. John Paul II develops the Genesis narrative, clarifying we are good despite Original Sin.

> In this context it is evident that original sin in Adam's descendants does not have the character of personal guilt. It is the privation of sanctifying grace in a nature which has been diverted from its supernatural end through the fault of the first parents.[4]

Christ comes, uniting humanity to divinity only to restore humanity back to its original dignity: filled with grace. This is St. John Paul II's great theme: the redemption of humanity as portrayed in his first encyclical: Redemptor Hominis.

> The redemption of the world—this tremendous mystery of love in which creation is renewed is, at its deepest root, the fullness of justice in a human heart—the Heart of the First-born Son—in order that it may become justice in the hearts of many human beings, predestined from eternity in the Firstborn Son to be children of God and called to grace, called to love. The Cross on Calvary,

---

2. John Paul II, "General Audience, October 29, 1986," sec. 9.

3. John Paul II, "General Audience, October 8, 1986," sec. 2.

4. John Paul II, "General Audience, October 8, 1986," sec. 2.

through which Jesus Christ—a Man, the Son of the Virgin Mary, thought to be the son of Joseph of Nazareth—"leaves" this world, is also a fresh manifestation of the eternal fatherhood of God, who in him draws near again to humanity, to each human being, giving him the thrice holy "Spirit of truth."[5]

Jesus' ultimate purpose regenerates what was lost. Because we have lost sanctifying grace, baptism into Christ regenerates us (DS 1514).[6] This comprehensive understanding of Original Sin explained by St. John Paul II offers a theological maturity, healing the person from shame. Mediocrity is the condition which allows us to live lives of neglect and carelessness of the truth, goodness, and dignity of who we truly are. Instead, realizing we are created good ought to drive us to restore our goodness through the gift offered by God himself: sanctifying grace.

LOVE'S VOCATION: RESTORING SANCTIFYING GRACE

Aquinas exploring God's character asks the most probing of questions, Does love exist in God? St. John Paul II develops and answers this idea telling us love is our fundamental vocation. Love satisfies our greatest desire: *communio*. It makes us fully human. Love's essence graces ourselves to the other as God graces himself to us. In this light, St. Thomas tries to correct a misconception that love is not free, but instead love is a uniting and binding force. In his pithy way, Aquinas explains:

> An act of love always tends towards two things; to the good that one wills, and to the person for whom one wills it: since to love a person is to wish that person good. Hence, inasmuch as we love ourselves, we wish ourselves good; and, so far as possible, union with that good. . . . And by the fact that anyone loves another, he wills good to that other. Thus he puts the other, as it were, in the place of himself.[7]

By the power of his love, God gifts and creates Adam and Eve from grace for God himself is Grace. Adorned with grace, Adam and Eve had the fullness of divine life. In essence they are another self of God, though

---

5. John Paul II, *Redemptor Hominis*, sec. 9.

6. DS abbreviates Denzinger, *Sources of Catholic Dogma*.

7. Aquinas, *Summa Theologica*, I.20.1, obj. 3.

created. Divine Goodness shares himself with us. The Son is the uncreated other self of God and when he incarnates, he puts himself in our fallen condition. In his perfect purity, he puts himself in our sinful state though he himself is sinless. This he does for one reason; he puts himself in our place so we can be placed in his presence again.

When we share ourselves, we too will the good to the other and we experience goodness within ourselves as Christ does. Shared goodness unites and completes us. On the other hand, self-centered love destroys goodness for it is not free. It is demanding. Demanding goodness from another creates a false self of empowerment making us ego-driven, trying to obtain the good of the other with force. It makes us inauthentic, destroying our true sense of transcendence, subjectivity, and openness to God by solely cultivating our self-determination.

The very nature of God, as St. John tells us, is love: God is love! (1 John 4:16). Love by its nature wills the good of the other bestowing fullness of being (Eph 3:19). Only in grace are we fully alive. Although grace, the gift of God's love, is freely given to all, no one is forced to accept the gift. We can reject love.

Satan inverts love from a gift to another, changing it to a gift to self. In that switch, love becomes forced and addictive. Concupiscence entices us to use the other, not value the other. This is the *incurvatus se* dilemma destroying friendship. St. John Paul II explains this. "Adam's sin has passed to all his descendants, that is, to all men and women as descendants of our first parents, and their heirs, in human nature already deprived of God's friendship."[8]

This loss, an alienation from God, is not a total deprivation. Original Sin, as the Council of Trent calls it, is the spark of sin; or as Augustine famously explains, sin is concupiscence and inclines us to sin (DS 1515). The Council of Orange expresses it as "the whole man, body, and soul has been thrown into confusion."[9]

Christ incarnates not merely to heal us of personal sin, which many now think. In fact, he came specifically to destroy the source of sin, Satan, and heal us of the consequences of the Fall, sin, and death. This is his creative and salvific will. He offers sanctifying grace so once again we may behold God's face. Without this grace, our wholeness is broken, and we are left to our whims and desires of our concupiscence which deceives

8. John Paul II, "General Audience, October 8, 1986."
9. John Paul II, "General Audience, October 8, 1986."

and manipulates our free will. Alienated, we are forced to sin. However, St. Pius IX defines the difference between Original Sin and Personal Sin. It is understood that no one is obliged to be in a state this sin. No one is forced to commit sin. Sin must be of free will. St. Pius IX declares this in *Quanto conficiamur moerore*:

> Because God knows, searches and clearly understands the minds, hearts, thoughts, and nature of all, his supreme kindness and clemency do not permit anyone at all who is not guilty of deliberate sin to suffer eternal punishments.[10]

That is why many who have been victimized through abuse, violence, along with those innocent victims who suffer the tragedies of unexpected death, are not condemned to hell as popular thought proports but belong to God in his merciful way.

How do we reconnect our free will with our divine goodness? If God declares we are good, we are not totally depraved and empty of all goodness! Love wills the good. We receive goodness because it is impossible to exist without some goodness within us. Aquinas states, "Augustine says (De Trin. vi 10) that the trace of the Trinity is found in every creature."[11]

God wills the goodness to the other and if I don't think I have any goodness within me, though we do by the sheer fact we exist, I will not receive and recognize the goodness given especially through forgiveness.

Original Sin diverts our fundamental vocation to find and gift love, turning it into a power to possess and dominate the love of the other. "In my fallen state, I define my own goodness; whether it is true or not, I decide." Yet Jesus Christ heals us of our fallen state. As St. John Paul II says, "Original sin must constantly be considered in reference to the mystery of the redemption carried out by Jesus Christ, the Son of God, who "for us men and for our salvation became man.""[12]

As we study and mature our understanding, St. John Paul II develops the Genesis narrative clarifying we are good despite Original Sin.

> In this context it is evident that original sin in Adam's descendants does not have the character of personal guilt. It is the privation

---

10. Pius IX, *Quanto*, sec. 7.

11. Aquinas, *Summa Theologica*, I.45.7.

12. John Paul II, "General Audience, Oct 8, 1986."

of sanctifying grace in a nature which has been diverted from its supernatural end through the fault of the first parents.[13]

Yet God's love heals, offering us his friends new sanctifying grace. Paul describes love as our hope:

> Love never ends. As for prophecies, they will pass away; as for tongues, they will cease; as for knowledge, it will pass away. For we know in part and we prophesy in part, but when the perfect comes, the partial will pass away. When I was a child, I spoke like a child, I thought like a child, I reasoned like a child. When I became a man, I gave up childish ways. For now we see in a mirror dimly, but then face to face. Now I know in part; then I shall know fully, even as I have been fully known. (1 Cor 13:8–12)

THE ETERNAL PROPHECY OF THE PROTOEVANGELIUM

God unleashes his power and presence immediately following the Fall as we read in Genesis 3:15 The Fall had left humanity injured and bleeding, deprived of sanctifying grace. In allegory, we say that the Fall denied the existence of God's essence. In tropology, morality, we say that the Fall denied the authority of God's will. In anagogy, we say that the Fall destroyed human destiny. Alienated from God the Father, the prophecy called the Protoevangelium plans the restoration. The whole plan of the Protoevangelium is to destroy the source of Original Sin and to restore us into original justice. In so doing, the source of personal sin is healed, and we are washed clean and sanctified by grace.

The Protoevangelium from Genesis 3:15 states.

> I will put enmity between you and the woman, and between your offspring and her offspring; he shall bruise your head, and you shall bruise his heel. (Gen 3:15)

The Fall impacted all of humanity following this divorce, but the prophecy contained in the Protoevangelium establishes a new Covenant. In the Fall, Adam and Eve broke the covenant and closed themselves to transcendence and friendship, focusing solely on their self-determination

---

13. John Paul II, "General Audience, Oct 8, 1986."

and subjectivity: or as Augustine writes, "heaved out of happiness."[14] God addresses this heaviness as he offers hope in this foundational prophetic phrase unstated but present in the Protoevangelium: A child will be born. He will be your descendant that will crush the skull of the deceiver and seducer.

In God's mercy, the promise of Restoration and regeneration begins. Having lost the capacity for friendship, humanity now engages in depravity, both objective and subjective, external and interior. Following this prophecy, every human action whether in accord with God's will or not, completes the restoration—the regeneration—because God brings goodness out of evil (Rom 8:28).

The mind of God planned this spiritual healing for the Fall from the very foundation of creation. In God's kindness and justice, he prepared both an individual and a universal way out of the bondage of evil. These prophecies and plans contained in the Sacred Scriptures came from a time and place "utterly beyond,"[15] to use the phrase of St. John Paul II. A time before created time, for Wisdom, co-eternal with the Trinity, created and laid these plans in the very constitution of the universe. In Ephesians we read of this plan for the fullness of time.

> In him we have redemption through his blood, the forgiveness of our trespasses, according to the riches of his grace, which he lavished upon us, in all wisdom and insight making known to us the mystery of his will, according to his purpose, which he set forth in Christ as a plan for the fullness of time, to unite all things in him, things in heaven and things on earth. (Eph 1:7–10)

Seeing humanity wounded and desolate, our Creator intervenes immediately to save humanity and to destroy and forever punish the one who caused humanity to fall, Satan. The prophecy says that from the very body of the Woman—her seed—would come a descendent who would destroy the Father of Lies and all his descendants.

God places enmity and hatred between the woman and the serpent, a hatred that will continue between the woman's descendants and the serpent's descendants (Rev 12:17). This hatred creates our hope because God himself promises ultimate victory when the Offspring of Eve will strike the head of the serpent and crush his skull, killing the snake and his lies.

14. Augustine, *Trinity*, 331.
15. John Paul II, *Artists*, sec. 15.

How is this prophecy applied? The Church Fathers saw the fulfillment of the Protoevangelium in the crucifixion.

Jesus Christ (the offspring of Eve) is raised on the tree as his instrument of death while the serpent, Satan, at the foot of the cross gloats over his ultimate destruction of humanity. Satan wants us to embrace the lies that we are irredeemable, incompetent, and pathetic creations of a hateful, vengeful, and ruthless God.

The plan allows Satan to strike the heel of the Offspring of Eve killing him in the crucifixion. This happens as Jesus Christ suffers in agony on the tree. The serpent thinks he has victory when Eve's Seed dies upon the tree for cursed are all who die on a tree (Deut 21:23).

But Satan fails to notice that the tree that Jesus Christ dies upon is not any tree, but the Tree of Life—Jacob's Ladder that comes down from heaven to rescue us from the Evil One. On the cross of the Tree of Life, Jesus Christ shows all humanity the Face of God, who prays and blesses us, even as he is being tortured and killed. This shows us the absolute transcendency of God's mercy.

Mary stands at the foot of the Cross, the woman clothed with the Sun with the moon under her feet (Rev 12:1). She prays as her seed—Christ—crushes sin, death, hell, and Satan himself. It is finished! What is finished? The gates of hell do not prevail. They do not withstand the power of the All-powerful one, Jesus Christ, who comes in disguise: he is God; but he is also man who crushes the skull of the Serpent on Golgotha and smashes the gates of hell and opens the gates of heaven.

The cross is the unlocking device of the gates, both heaven and hell. The sacrifice of Christ on the cross becomes the fruit of the Tree of Life, giving sanctifying grace to all who obey as did Mary. In her role as the Arc of the New Covenant, Mary participates in recreating the Temple, the Garden of Eden called now the New Jerusalem.

Who could have thought a young woman Mary would take on the power of the Angel of Light, when Adam, a great priest and King, refused; when Eve the great queen of all the living was deceived by Angel of Light who becomes the Angel of Death?

Mary's victory over Satan humiliated him and continues throughout history. In Revelation 12, after Satan is thrown down to the earth, we face our only decision: will we serve? Will we offer the sacrifice of praise: our right worship of God?

St. Irenaeus describes the relationship between Eve and Mary. As sin entered because of Eve, so sin is destroyed through the New Eve: the Mother of Christ.

> But Eve was disobedient; . . . having become disobedient, was made the cause of death, both to herself and to the entire human race; so also did Mary, having a man betrothed to her, and being nevertheless a virgin, by yielding obedience, become the cause of salvation both to herself and the whole human race.[16]

Mary, as St. Irenaeus tells us, is *Causa Salutis*: cause of our salvation! As St. John Paul II explains, Mary, the New Woman, brings forth life—not death!

> Thus the Blessed Virgin advanced in her pilgrimage of faith, and faithfully persevered in her union with her Son unto the cross. There she stood, in keeping with the divine plan, enduring with her only begotten Son the intensity of his suffering, joining herself with his sacrifice in her mother's heart, and lovingly consenting to the immolation of this victim, born of her: to be given, by the same Christ Jesus dying on the cross, as a mother to his disciple, with these words: "Woman, behold your son."[17]

Jesus begotten of God the Father and born of Mary honors our existence with respect and dignity loving us by redeeming and ransoming us from the snares of the Father of Lies. By adopting human existence, Jesus knew intense suffering in the crucifixion with pain, hunger, thirst, tears, frustration, and anger, all the states of being that we suffer. His heel was bitten by the serpent, but Jesus Christ in his suffering, displays pure humility, and wins victory, humiliating the one who humiliated us on that fateful day of the Fall, we now call the Protoevangelium: the Most Happiest of Faults.

This plan restores what was lost: the priesthood, the temple, the Covenant, and the friendship we had through sanctifying grace. The Protoevangelium reveals the way to a new friendship and union with God. St. John Paul II quotes St. Louis de Montfort on our Christian hope.

> If we live in Jesus and Jesus lives in us, we need not fear damnation. Neither angels in heaven nor men on earth, nor devils in hell,

16. Irenaeus, *Against Heresies*, 3.22.4.
17. *Catechism*, sec. 964.

no creature whatever can harm us, for no creature can separate us
from the love of God which is in Christ.[18]

God's plan for the restoration of human beings brings victory. Eve's
offspring, Christ, the Son of God, became the great high priest. In obediential suffering, Jesus restores sanctifying grace. This is the sacrifice of
praise enveloping us in our ecstatic recreated state: "Through him then let
us continually offer up a sacrifice of praise to God, that is, the fruit of lips
that acknowledge his name" (Heb 13:15). His crucifixion gifts us sanctifying and charismatic grace. Through these graces, we too, sanctified, serve
obediently.

The final confrontation between the forces of good and evil ends the
horrors and tragedy of the Fall. Christus vincit! Satan's temptations of Adam
and Eve caused the Fall of all humanity. God had put into place enmity between the serpent and Eve, along with enmity between the offspring of the
serpent and the offspring of Eve. Yet the promise rings out that an offspring
of Eve will strike the head of the serpent, while the offspring of the serpent
will strike the heel of the man, killing the human. Unbeknownst to the
serpent, the Human Being, Jesus Christ, rises from this physical death. In
this confrontation, the evil of Satan and his fallen angels will be destroyed
forever. The confrontation will only be won by the great sacrifice of the
Offspring of Eve, Mary, who engages with the horrific powers of darkness
of Satan.

PERSONAL REFLECTION: A CHANGED WORLD

I was standing on the corner of Piazza Venezia, the heart and center of
Rome. Above me was the window where Benito Mussolini spoke and united Italy into a Fascist Government. This piazza is the center of the whole
Italian nation. That day December 2, 1989, traffic stopped. Buses, cars, and
taxis all exited the Piazza as I was waiting for my bus. Then the carabinieri
motorcyclists led the motorcade through the piazza. Dozens of police es-
corts riding, sirens blaring, led several black limousines followed by more
police cars and motorcycles. There I was dumbfounded as to who was in
that motorcade. They don't shut down Piazza Venezia for anyone. The black
tinted windows covered up whoever it was, but whoever it was, had to be

18. John Paul II, *Jesus Sent*, sec. 5.

the most important person yet during my seven year stay in Rome. Upset that my bus was not on time, I had to walk home.

That night on the evening news, Italian television shows St. John Paul II on the screen. He was joking and conversing casually with all the media personal. Then the cameras turned, and Mikhail Gorbachev walked into the screen. Immediately, St. John Paul II turned, smiled seriously, and offered his hand. The man who succeeded Josef Stalin now stood in front of the man, St. John Paul II, who had survived the holocaust, the purging of intellectuals and artist by both atheistic regimes, the "cleansing" of the clergy by the atheists, and attacks on human dignity and personal freedom.

The meeting was not adversarial. It was not even a peace treaty. It was a meeting to reconcile a century worth of sin, slavery, and oppression: to open the doors and break down the walls. This historic moment changed history. The man who lived in Poland under Russian Communism broke communism and its hold on Poland, Czechoslovakia, Hungry, Romania and the rest of the eastern bloc nations. That year, all of Europe was in awe as the Berlin Wall fell and human dignity and personal freedom, especially freedom to express one's faith, was restored.

Evil is unrecognizable when we deny the transcendent dignity of who we are. We misunderstand the power and persuasion of evil. Not a mere simplistic misbehavior, evil completely rejects the Divine Beauty of God the Father who seeks to perfect us by correcting our faults. Evil at its root rejects the essence of relationships: the giving and receiving of the gift of love through the power of the Holy Spirit. Sin opposes gift love as St. John Paul II describes the dark forces of extreme evil.

> This expression, which echoes what St. Paul writes concerning the mystery of evil, helps us to grasp the obscure and intangible element hidden in sin. Clearly sin is a product of man's freedom. But deep within its human reality there are factors at work which place it beyond the merely human, in the border area where man's conscience, will and sensitivity are in contact with the dark forces which, according to St. Paul, are active in the world almost to the point of ruling it.[19]

Evil easily rules our consciences. We lust for powers, pleasures, and possessions especially when we face the injustices of raw power: the abuse of others for self-gratification, and the crippling poverty amidst the wealth.

---

19. John Paul II, *Reconciliation*, sec. 14.

Blinded by evil, we react emotionally attacking the abuses with the same mindset that caused the abuses.

> When people think they possess the secret of a perfect social organization which makes evil impossible, they also think that they can use any means, including violence and deceit, in order to bring that organization into being. Politics then becomes a 'secular religion' which operates under the illusion of creating paradise in this world.[20]

The new thinking needed to solve the problem of evil is not human, it is divine. This new thinking that St. Paul describes as the mystery of evil, which St. John Paul II lived, needs a new conqueror, Jesus Christ. The Catechism reads, "We must therefore approach the question of the origin of evil by fixing the eyes of our faith on him who alone is its conqueror."[21]

20. John Paul II, *Centesimus Annus*, sec. 25.
21. *Catechism*, sec. 385.

Chapter Six

THE THIRD STEP
Metanoia: Facing Death

IN METANOIS, OUR MIND and heart yearn to be with our Creator, our Father, and we keep his face continually before us in prayer. We sense the movement of the Spirit in an interior still, small voice, almost imperceptible. But in our passion to behold the Beatific Vision, we adapt our lives to live in ways that draw us closer to God and bring out more fully the inscrutable vision of the Trinity given to us all. St. John Paul II calls all to holiness through the perfecting power of metanoia. "Holiness, a message that convinces without the need for words, is the living reflection of the face of Christ."[1] In this third step of theosis, our metanoia happens under the power of the message of holiness.

Catholic mystic Madame Guyon describes the mystery of metanoia.

> A loving heart can find a way:
> When we follow Love, we fear no danger.
> When we look lost and desolate, in most dreadful paths, yet the
> soul finds its way.
> We pass through any experience.[2]

We see this in the life of St. John Paul II. On February 18, 1941 the dark loneliness of death left Karol Wojtyla empty: "I never felt so alone."[3]

---

1. John Paul II, *Novo Millennio*, sec. 7.
2. Guyon, *Divine Love*, 101.
3. Quoted in Weigel, *Witness*, 68.

The senior Karol was homebound for some time, the younger Karol would come home from work and sit with his father. He became his confidant as his mother died at an early age and his brother died some years before. That night when he and his friend Juliusz Kydrynski came home to prepare the evening dinner for the elder Karol, the son found his father dead.

Death leaves us deserted and when parents die, we feel the abandonment of God. We become orphans. All death mirrors the death of Adam and Eve when they ate of the tree and found out they were naked, divorced from God and isolated from each other. They felt forsaken. When we face the death of a child, a parent, or a spouse, we too experience the emptiness of life. In fact, our life ends as we know it when death strikes.

The power of death draws life out of us, and we become so alone—lonely—longing for that companionship. Death carries no hope of reconciliation. There is no bringing back to life is there? Or maybe, just maybe, there is the hope of the resurrection. Instead of asking why death exists, delving deeper through theosis, we change the question and ask: Why is there life?

Karol's emptiness drove him closer to God—not farther as it does so many. With his father's death, he searched for the meaning of his life, despite the evils he was living in: Poland became the pawn of Nazi Germany and Communist Russia. His personal history set the stage for the most incredible victory of the 20th Century.

Metanoia conquers and gives incredible victories. St. John Paul II says that the face of Christ reflects pure holiness.

> "When we cry 'Abba, Father!', it is the Spirit himself bearing witness with our spirit that we are children of God" (*Rm* 8:15–16). Here we are at the centre of the mystery! It is in the meeting between the Holy Spirit and the human spirit that we find the very heart of what the Apostles experienced at Pentecost. This extraordinary experience is present in the Church born of that event and accompanies her down the centuries.
>
> Under the Holy Spirit's action, man fully discovers that his spiritual nature is not veiled by corporeity but, on the contrary, it is his spirit which gives true meaning to his body. Indeed, by living according to the Spirit, he fully manifests the gift of his adoption as a son of God.[4]

---

4. John Paul II, *Solemnity of Pentecost*, sec. 3.

As John Paul II says, the Face of Christ reflects to us living holiness. We have seen the Father's Face in the face of Jesus, the perfect reflection of the Father's love revealed to us through his Spirit. In metanoia, this awareness penetrates our minds as it did with Abraham and Sarah, as it does with St. John Paul II because the perfection of heaven calls from the edge of our consciousness.

To bring forth the goodness of metanoia, Jesus accompanies us, the great pastoral approach of St. John Paul II. He, as did Jesus, interacts with the whole person, not to be judgmental or moralistic, but to listen, understand, and create metanoia. He walks with the person, listens, and empathizes with our struggles. Accompaniment cares for the whole person, especially the parts ridden with evil. Seeing beyond the sin, accompaniment transforms us into an icon of beauty. Walking with our Confidant, we see the beauty of his meekness and humility. He conquers our ego by offering friendship: a restored communion with the *Communio Personarum*.

This is metanoia, the third stage of theosis. We open our heart and listen to the Divine Counselor who breaks into our consciousness and we experience his presence offering us his mercy. His gratuitous gift of mercy reveals and forgives the gravity of sin, as sin separates us from our communion and friendship with the Father. In our response to this great gift, our interior life shifts and transforms, bringing us to a new and powerful *communio* with God.

Accompaniment calls us back to be in full communion with the Father, through the forgiveness of the Son. This is the drama of the *Communio Personarum*. It is our personal choice if we accept the invitation or not. In death we need accompaniment to lead us out of the pain, loss, grief, and anger.

Metanoia brings light into our dark, mental space. This is the purpose of metanoia: to change and transform our mind and heart.

Peter preaches about metanoia. God accompanies us on our journey and because of this we no longer fear. "Repent (Greek μετανοειτε = metanoia) and believe in the gospel" (Mark 1:15).

Pope Paul VI teaches about metanoia.

> "Repent and believe in the Gospel." These words constitute, in a way, a compendium of the whole Christian life. The kingdom of God announced by Christ can be entered only by a "change of heart" ("metanoia") that is to say through that intimate and total change and renewal of the entire man—of all his opinions,

judgments and decisions—which takes place in him in the light of the sanctity and charity of God, the sanctity and charity which were manifested to us in the Son and communicated fully.[5]

Paul's Letter to the Galatians describes the spiritual gifts given to us in metanoia.

Love, joy, peace, patience, kindness, goodness, faithfulness, gentleness, self-control; against such things there is no law. And those who belong to Christ Jesus have crucified the flesh with its passions and desires (Gal 5:22).

In our struggle for divine righteousness, we suffer. But we do not suffer in vain. We suffer out of love. Love gives meaning to suffering and love embraces the battles not out of egoism, but out of humility to perfect our imperfections. Sufferings sculpt our fallen and broken self-image back into its beautiful state! St. John Paul II says that to become transcendent, we must suffer.

What we express by the word "suffering" seems to be particularly essential to the nature of man. It is as deep as man himself, precisely because it manifests in its own way that depth which is proper to man, and in its own way surpasses it. Suffering seems to belong to man's transcendence: it is one of those points in which man is in a certain sense "destined" to go beyond himself, and he is called to this in a mysterious way.[6]

What person would not struggle against evil if they knew that their perfection was guaranteed? What man would not work, toil, and labor if he knew that in the end, his efforts were embraced with a perfect love of his bride? What woman would not endure the pains of pregnancy and pour herself out raising her children if she knew that, along with her bridegroom, they would receive eternal love?

What religious or priest consecrated to Jesus would not exhaust themselves for the community, parish, rising early, praying fervently, and contemplating deeply the mysteries dwelling within the scriptures knowing that divine beauty and perfection will be poured into the thirsting soul worshipping and waiting?

We do this daily in metanoia. We seek an abundant life, living our call to communion. The essential question of metanoia is: What kingdom do I

5. Paul VI, *Paenitemini*, sec. 34
6. John Paul II, *Salvifici Doloris*, sec. 2.

seek? Jesus tells us seek first his kingdom and the rest will be given (Matt 6:33). God's Kingdom alone satisfies the deepest longings of our heart. But this is our struggle: to stay faithful to his way—not our way.

When we submit to Christ and his grace, then we are wrapped with the armor of God, his goodness, beauty, and truth. He enfolds us in his unconditional love knowing that whatever we face, he comes again and again restoring us. Our battle scars endured in metanoia, as those of Christ's passion, reveal our victory over evil.

Embracing these scars, a result of our sufferings, we will never despair or grow weary when we enter combat with evil and the Evil One. Our victory is guaranteed, knowing that God's grace is sufficient to restore our ugliness into divine beauty.

In metanoia, Jesus, Divine Beauty Incarnate, dwells within and sanctifies our soul. We cling to him, knowing his mercy is always greater than our sin.

THE ESSENCE OF BEAUTY: CHRIST'S CRUCIFIXION

What is beauty? The Via Pulchritudino documents this for us.

> [Beauty] expresses a certain power of attraction, beauty tells forth reality itself in the perfection of its form. It is its epiphany. It manifests it by expressing its internal brightness. If the good speaks the desirable, the beautiful tells forth the splendor and light of the perfection it manifests.[7]

The beauty of the Cross of Christ is the Christian Paradox. On the cross, the reality of Jesus Christ's pain and suffering repulses anyone who dares to look. Upon the cross, Jesus suffers humiliation and shame. Nothing is left for the imagination for the passion, crucifixion, and death of Jesus bares the face of absolute ugliness. Yet, instead of being a Roman Execution, the crucifixion of Christ becomes the Sacred Mystery: the Icon of Gift Love. On this instrument of torture, Jesus embraces his cross and upon it, declares to all, Father Forgive them. Forgiveness and love create within us the heart of metanoia. "God shows his love for us in that while we were still sinners, Christ died for us" (Rom 5:8).

The whole purpose of Divine Beauty becoming visible in the Face of Jesus transforms the entire human existence. *Misericordia*, literally a

---

7. Benedict XVI, *Via Pulchritudinis*, II.2.

miserable heart, actually is accompaniment. We partake of another's suffering, not just to endure the pain, but to comfort. Comfort shares strength.
Christ shares his strength with us comforting us for his heart embraces our
suffering.

Sin is selfishness, *incurvatus se*. Jesus inverts this turning inward by
offering himself through his mercy, misericordia. Mercy is given to all, but
not all are open to it. To experience metanoia, one chooses to change the
focus of their heart. No longer is it self-centered but God centered. This is
the true beauty of the Cross. We see the cross as an expression of pure love.

Jesus pours his self-gifting love into our humanity broken by selfishness; and in so doing, we are recreated into his image and likeness. We now
partake of the divine for the very Divine Life abides in me and I abide in
him through this mysterious Bread and Wine. And so, sin and death no
longer have hold over us for his sacrificial love has cut us free.

True beauty reflects our original beauty, and the crucifixion of Christ
displays the paradox of divine beauty. In this contradiction, the pure ugliness of sin awakens in us the yearning for divine beauty. Jesus is incarnate
Beauty and re-establishes our beauty. On the cross, the secret ladder, Jesus
is lifted up. Pope Benedict explains,

> The coming of the Redeemer re-establishes man in his first beauty;
> moreover, it redresses him in a new beauty: the unimaginable
> beauty of the creature raised up to divine sonship, the transfigura-
> tion promised by the soul ransomed and lifted up by Grace, re-
> splendent in all its fiber, the body called to new life.[8]

Through his passion, Jesus changes death into life. He exchanges
his life for ours and the execution of Jesus becomes the gift of new life—
grace—to be recreated. That is why he tells us to do this in his memory. Do
what? "Truly, truly, I say to you, unless you eat the flesh of the Son of Man
and drink his blood, you have no life in you. Whoever feeds on my flesh
and drinks my blood has eternal life, and I will raise him up on the last day"
(John 6:53–54).

Only the beautiful attracts us and as Augustine expresses beauty is
love. He ties beauty and love together in a wonderful knot, "*Non possumus
amare, nisi pulchra?* (What can we love, if not beauty?)[9] The Beauty of the

---

8. Benedict XVI, *Via Pulchritudinis*, III.1.B.

9. Augustine, *De musica*, 6,13, 38.

crucifixion reveals the depth of divine love and calls us through Jesus, The Crucified One, to experience metanoia and love sacrificially.

We receive the fullness of divine life as St. Irenaeus profoundly annunciates, *Visio Dei, vita hominis*: "Man's life consists in the vision of God."[10] Man is fully alive when he sees the Love of Christ on the cross reflecting his own divine beauty.

THE ICON AS INCARNATION

How do we experience the beauty of incarnate love? St. John Paul describes icons as a fresh experience of the Incarnation, which makes the power of the Son of God present among us anew. The Nicaean Council settled the iconoclast controversy by deciding that the icon could be a sensory evocation of the mystery of the incarnation. St. John Paul II writes, "If the Son of God had come into the world of visible realities . . . building a bridge between the visible and invisible . . . by analogy, a representation of the mystery could be used within the light of signs as a sensory evocation of the mystery."[11] In this bridge between immanent and transcendent realities, we may receive the blessings of sparks of light from heaven (allegory), the idea of a righteous action (tropology) or a sense of our ultimate destiny (anagogy).

A powerful icon showers new life upon us, connecting us with transcendent realities. The icon represents the inscrutable mystery of the Son of God and invites us into a profound communion with the transcendent mystery. With our hearts and mind worshipping, we receive within our being the sense of *communio*, of being enveloped with beauty, of participating and loving the community of saints. In this vision, divine transcendence warms us with sparks of light from the beyond.

The power of icons points beyond itself, and in our journey of theosis, the icon welcomes our ascension closer to the Beatific Vision as if calling, "Come, O Blessed of my Father"(Matt 25:34). St. John Paul II concludes, "In a sense, the icon is a sacrament. By analogy with what occurs in the sacraments, the icon makes present the mystery of the Incarnation in one of other of its aspects."[12]

10. Irenaeus, *Against Heresies*, IV.20.7, quoted in John Paul II, "General Audience, April 5, 2000," sec. 5.

11. John Paul II, *Artists*, sec. 7.

12. John Paul II, *Artists*, sec. 8.

Celebrating the passion, death, and resurrection of Christ through the liturgy of an icon restores our beauty. Through the Spirit, we pray the sacrifice of true praise. Like the wine in the Holy Eucharist, our water of humanity mingles with the wine of Jesus' divinity. We may partake of his divinity as he humbled himself to share in our humanity. Pope Benedict writes of this mystery of redemption.

> Liturgy is not what man does but is a divine work. The faithful need to be helped to perceive that the act of worship is not the fruit of activity, a product, a merit, a gain, but is the expression of a mystery, of something that cannot be entirely understood but that needs to be received rather than conceptualized. It is an act entirely free from considerations of efficiency. The attitude of the believer in the liturgy is marked by its capacity to receive, a condition of the progress of the spiritual life.[13]

In the Sacred Liturgy, we participate in the fullness of Divine Revelation, revealing the mystery of the transcendent. Sacred Beauty transfigures us, and we are annihilated, emptied of all that is not pure. The pouring of the water into wine at the offertory during the Sacred Liturgy symbolizes this theosis: we are enfolded into Our Father's heart. Receiving the fullness and mystery of the Divine Life at Mass, we too are resurrected for the crucified Christ now dwells in our soul. In our worship, we bow and adore his Divine Charity knowing, "Wherever charity shines forth, the beauty that saves is manifest."[14]

What is the most beautiful then? The crucifixion of Jesus Christ is. How is this possible? It leads to the complete conversion as Augustine experienced. Feeling the power of his sin, blinded by sin, Augustine experiences God's love.

> Late have I loved you, O beauty, so old and so new, too late have I loved you! You were here and I sought elsewhere; I was deformed, drowning in those fair forms you made. . . . You called. You shouted. You battered my deafness. You shone. You glistened. You shattered my blindness. You radiated and I breathed in your spirit, and I desired you. I tasted you and hungered, thirsted after you. You touched me and I burned for your peace.[15]

13. Benedict XVI, *Via Pulchritudinis*, III.3.C.
14. Benedict XVI, *Via Pulchritudinis*, III.3.B.
15. Augustine, *Confessions*, X.27.

In recollection, the heart of the liturgy, Jesus tells us to do this in his memory. We remember what he did not as a past event, but as present, alive in our hearts. We too are touched by the burning love of Divine Beauty and humbly accept our metanoia.

CATHOLIC RECONCILIATION

What happens with us still living in the consequences of the Fall? In our Catholic faith, we have another place of restoration: Reconciliation. Confession is a life-changing moment. In our guilt and traumas, our fears and even horrors, we seek out Christ, through the priest, to confide in, seeing in him as our confidant. The priest, endowed with the power of the Holy Spirit cleanses, heals, and consoles. In the darkness of the confessional revealing and exposing our hearts, we leave enlightened, experiencing the absolute love of our Divine Confidant.

If we refuse the confession, out of shame, embarrassment, or fear of vulnerability, our sorrows increase. Sin may become our master. Without the actual admittance of my own fault, we no longer feel grounded. Isolated, we may live as outcasts in a strange physical, emotional, and spiritual dark space because we live by our human impulses with their innate, immature instincts.

As the scriptures witness, the voice of the serpent embedded deep within our nature feeds our animalistic nature. Take the broad way, the easy path, blind to the coming destruction, failing to separate ourselves first from seduction then the corruption of sin. St. John Paul II describes this dread reality.

> Human "evil" constituted by the Evil One or instigated by him is also presented in our time in an attractive form that seduces minds and hearts so as to cause the very sense of evil and sin to be lost. It is a question of that "mystery of evil" of which St Paul speaks (cf. 2 *Thes* 2:7).[16]

Evil, St. Augustine ponders, "I sought whence it come and there was not solution."[17] Pondering evil leads to despair if our minds do not grasp the mystery of Divine Beauty. Evil is the lack of beauty. It is the complete disfigurement of the beautiful. With the Fall, we experience the desolation

---

16. John Paul II, "General Audience, August 18, 1999," sec. 4.

17. Augustine, *Confessions*, 7.7.11; *Catechism*, sec. 385.

of this world. Yet Jesus' call to all of us still lingers in our consciousness, "Come and see" (John 1:39). Be united with Me!

THE BEAUTY OF FRIENDSHIP

In metanoia, divine beauty creates the goodness of friendship within us. Friendship creates interior openness to the depths of the soul. It builds trust for each friend seeks the perfection of the other. Friendship reigns leading us on the way to truth and life.

> The light of God's face shines in all its beauty on the countenance of Jesus Christ, "the image of the invisible God" (*Col* 1:15), the "reflection of God's glory" (*Heb* 1:3), "full of grace and truth" (*Jn* 1:14). Christ is "the way, and the truth, and the life" (*Jn* 14:6).[18]

Beauty, the countenance of Jesus Christ, welcomes us into friendship with him. His beauty covers our nakedness and shame, clothing us with the light of glory, honor, and splendor. Beauty attracts us, then creates integrity within uniting both our body and soul into a unified whole in which our bodies become the indwelling of the Holy Spirit. As St. Thomas Aquinas defines, Jesus is the most perfect expression of this beauty:

> Species or beauty has a likeness to the property of the Son. For beauty includes three conditions, "integrity" or "perfection," since those things which are impaired are by the very fact ugly; due "proportion" or "harmony"; and lastly, "brightness" or "clarity," whence things are called beautiful which have a bright color.[19]

Integrity—perfection—comes from the image and likeness of what it represents. Created in the image and likeness of God, Jesus at the incarnation perfectly reflects God and man in his human and divine natures united into one Person. In his incarnation, Jesus comes to perfect us. Living outside the truth of who we are in Christ, we lose our integrity, harmony, and clarity. Yet we find the mystery of integrity in our friendships guided by morality. Friendship—receiving from the other and then personally choosing to be good, truthful, and beautiful to the other for it is who I am—reveals our goodness as a person and makes us radiant with divine life.

The three transcendentals of truth, goodness, and beauty interrelate. God's beauty draws us closer; and when we dwell in his beauty, we yearn

18. John Paul II, *Veritatis*, sec. 2.

19. Aquinas, *Summa Theologica*, I.39.8.

more profoundly for God's goodness which creates friendship. We know the passion of God for human righteousness. Living the moral actions, choosing to be personally responsible to another person for our own actions, we sense order and symmetry: integrity. His friendship creates our personal righteousness because he relates to us personally not as an abstract deity, but as a Person whose image we reflect. Our reflection of the clarity or radiance of the divine image makes us whole.

Our God, Jesus, becomes exactly like us to reveal to us who we are to become. We are to relate to the Father's invitation to friendship with him through the Son and Spirit.

Many, as did the Rich Young Man, have a profound desire for God's friendship: his acceptance and love. Our deep desire for this *communio* reveals to us our *solitudino personarum*, our loneliness. Everyone needs another; we are made for another, to unite physically, emotionally, mentally, and spiritually. We call this union friendship. But for friendship to be free, it must be guided by the goodness of morality. Morality frees us to live in the spirit. It is not the goal, but the foundation for loving friendships.

> Jesus, then, is the living, personal summation of perfect freedom in total obedience to the will of God. His crucified flesh fully reveals the unbreakable bond between freedom and truth, just as his Resurrection from the dead is the supreme exaltation of the fruitfulness and saving power of a freedom lived out in truth.[20]

Love and do what you will, says Augustine. Why? Because true friendship has no boundaries. It is free and limitless. Friendship liberates for it wills the beauty, grace, and friendship of the other. This is the only choice that sets us free: mutual benevolence as Aquinas expounds. "Love which is together with benevolence, when, to wit, we love someone so as to wish good to him."[21] Friendship is the heart of charity for it communicates, mutual *benevolentia*: the very truth, goodness, and beauty of the other.

Love and do what you want, then, spends ourselves to ensure the other becomes who they are meant to be: the best version of our self. This is the law of freedom that St. Paul reveals to us, "For you were called to freedom, brothers. Only do not use your freedom as an opportunity for the flesh, but through love serve one another" (Gal 5:13). Love lived in freedom mutually wills the good of the other, building true friendship. Anything else fails.

20. John Paul II, *Veritatis*, sec. 87.
21. Aquinas, *Summa Theologica*, II-II.23.1.

> It is possible to build up a friendship on the basis of this present
> of God's communication, *fundari amicitiam* ("build up a friend-
> ship"). If there is a phrase that sums up the entire Summa Theolog-
> ica, it is in my opinion *fundari amicitiam*. God wishes to build up
> a friendship with his creation. The whole way of human Christian
> life has its deepest sense in the building of friendship with God.[22]

Fundari amicitiam is the sheer gift that betters the other. It wills the
good of the other solely for the benefit of the other—never for self!

God befriends us willing our goodness, for his Paradise is our heart.
The question arises, Is his Heart our paradise? Open to receive his goodness, truth, and beauty identifies who we are. We are his; we are his other
self in this friendship. Jesus proclaims his friendship and willingness to give
himself to us, but if we want to be friends with him, we must be willing to
receive and return *benevolentia* as he commands,

> Greater love has no one than this, that someone lay down his life
> for his friends. You are my friends if you do what I command you.
> No longer do I call you servants, for the servant does not know
> what his master is doing; but I have called you friends, for all that
> I have heard from my Father I have made known to you. (John
> 15:13–15)

Jesus gives us his all. St. Paul experiencing the friendship of Jesus on
the Damascus Road explains Jesus' invitation to friendship: He who did
not spare his own Son but gave him up for us all, how will he not also with
him graciously give us all things? (Rom 8:32). How does Christ love us? He
gives us all things, everything he has is ours! The whole of creation groans
for God's friendship though he entrusted all of creation to our care. We
then are to be friends—good stewards—of creation.

Jesus commands our friendship to love God, inspiring us to echo true
participation as the Great Shema proclaims. "Hear, O Israel: The Lord our
God, the Lord is one. You shall love the Lord your God with all your heart
and with all your soul and with all your might (Deut 6:4–5). In the Garden, God gave Adam and Eve everything commanding them not to destroy
his friendship with them. After the Fall, God gave the command again to
love him beyond all the other goodness we derive from our friendships or
our concupiscence for creation. Without a *communio*: a personal, heart to
heart, face to face friendship with God as Father, Jesus as Brother, Holy
Spirit as expressed love, we seek satisfaction solely in earthly friendships.

22. Schönborn, "On Love and Friendship."

But these are meant to lead us to God; they should not be the focus of our friendships. They express God's desire for our friendship with him.

Why would we not want a friendship with God? Why would we not want all that God possesses? Without friendship with God, we become like Adam, *solitudino personae*. We are alone. Isolated we never submit because sin speaks to the sinner (Ps 36) and in our sin the face of God is hidden (Ps 44). Darkness becomes my only companion as Psalm 88 reveals, and we become victims afflicted with loneliness.

Theosis, then, prays to seek the hidden face of God. It unveils the mystery of self-donation. Inviting us to participate fully in God's friendship, as fully as a human person can. Jesus summons—even tempts us—to embrace his very self as friend. Friendship with God fulfills our deepest longings for *communio*.

This is fulfillment of the command that blesses us: May the Glory of God unveil your heart so after kindled in the fire of divine love, all that is pure beauty, grace, and friendship, revealing the connection between charity and friendship. Friendship love is the heart of *Communio Personarum*.

Chapter Seven

THE FOURTH STEP
The New Pentecost

ST. JOHN PAUL II says that the original Pentecost burst into human history, and its active outpouring still continues, blessing us with meaning and power. In his address to those gathered studying the implementation of the council he advocates.

> The Second Vatican Ecumenical Council has been a gift of the Spirit to his Church. For this reason it remains a fundamental event not only for understanding the Church's history at this end of the century, but first and foremost for exploring the abiding presence of the risen Christ beside his Bride in the course of world events. Through the Council Assembly, which saw Bishops come to the See of Peter from all over the world, it was possible to note how the patrimony of 2,000 years of faith has been preserved in its original authenticity.
>
> 2. With the Council, *the Church first had an experience of faith*, as she abandoned herself to God without reserve, as one who trusts and is certain of being loved. It is precisely this act of abandonment to God which stands out from an objective examination of the Acts. Anyone who wished to approach the Council without considering this interpretive key *would be unable to penetrate its depths*. Only from a faith perspective can we see the Council event as a gift whose still hidden wealth we must know how to mine.[1]

1. John Paul II, "Implementation," sec. 1, 2.

In theosis we live in spiritual humility and docility following the inspirations of the Holy Spirit. The New Pentecost then restores us by seeing God's Heart imprinted upon our soul, for we have been blessed by beauty from within. After our metanoia, this is the fourth step in theosis: the New Pentecost. St. John XXIII began the Second Vatican Council with holy prayers for a New Pentecost.

> Renew Your wonders in this our day, as by a new Pentecost. Grant to Your Church that, being of one mind and steadfast in prayer with Mary, the Mother of Jesus, and following the lead of blessed Peter, it may advance the reign of our Divine Savior, the reign of truth and justice, the reign of love and peace. Amen.[2]

At the Second Vatican Council, the whole world was amazed. Anew, the Spirit was breathing forth from this enclosed institution known as the Catholic Church. The winds of the Holy Spirit were gently breathing and the sails of the souls of many believers, especially the bishops of the of the Council, were inspired to breathe anew the Spirit into the life of the Church.

St. Pope John XXIII on January 25, 1959, called for a Council to renew the face of the Church. He became the originator of this call for a New Pentecost along with Joseph Ratzinger (Pope Benedict XVI) and others, including St. John Paul II who attended the council as a newly ordained bishop.

The Catholic Church, the body of Christ, is not made with bricks and mortar; She is not merely dogmas and doctrines; She is not a set of traditions and rituals, though this is what most onlookers believe. No, the Church is more than these. She is the One, Holy, Mystical Body of Christ made up with many members who receive the gift of Divine Life—the Pentecost—at their Christian Initiation: Baptism, Confirmation, and the Holy Eucharist.

Christ, the Bridegroom, promises to send his Spirit to teach us all things: "I will ask the Father, and he will give you another Helper, to be with you forever, even the Spirit of truth, whom the world cannot receive, because it neither sees him nor knows him. You know him, for he dwells with you and will be in you" (John 14:16–17). This Helper re-creates us. The Holy Spirit breathes new life into deprived—not completely depraved—creation. The Helper Spirit restores the ultimate meaning to our deprived

---

2. John XXIII, "Opening Address," sec. 23.

lives. Jesus comes calling his disciples into a *communio*, preparing them to receive the New Pentecost because they tasted his Divine Spirit.

Breathing new life into souls gasping for life, we too seek *communio* with the Divine. The Spirit breathes contemplation in us revealing we are bone of divine bone and flesh of divine flesh. These words, not taken literally, are taken nuptially. The Divine Confidant wants to restore our perfection by re-uniting us through the gifting of his Spirit though a spousal covenant.

Since the Fall from Gift Love, the Divine Artisan redesigns creation, seeking to make all things new: all creation, man, woman, and the universe are groaning for perfection. In the Garden is the Tree of Knowledge which is comprehensive knowledge; and comprehensive knowledge contains divine power; and divine power demands divine responsibility, which we humans do not self-possess. Yet, we easily seize Divine Knowledge claiming it as our own.

The Spirit through Christian Initiation re-orders our knowledge giving us those theological virtues—gifts—faith, hope, and charity. They open us to experience the dynamic presence of the Spirit. In this dynamism, we envision the Divine Truth, faith. Hope unveils the future, always calling to invite us into the Beatific Vision. The Charity of God penetrates our heart, pours forth his Divine Presence. With these, God clothes us and we radiate Divine Life. The mysteries from the foundation of the world beckon to us from that which is utterly beyond. As baptized, we live in the mystical body of Christ, overflowing with the Holy Spirit

> Now you are the body of Christ and individually members of it. And God has appointed in the church first apostles, second prophets, third teachers, then miracles, then gifts of healing, helping, administrating, and various kinds of tongues. Are all apostles? Are all prophets? Are all teachers? Do all work miracles? Do all possess gifts of healing? Do all speak with tongues? Do all interpret? But earnestly desire the higher gifts. (1 Cor 12:27–31)

Baptized by one Spirit, we all drink of one Spirit. Pope Benedict XVI addressing the Charismatic Movement building on St. Paul's theology defines the New Pentecost as a living reality for those imbued with the Spirit, crying out for new charisms to enliven the Catholic Church.

> What we learn in the New Testament on charisms, which appeared as visible signs of the coming of the Holy Spirit, is not a historical event of the past, but a reality ever alive. It is the same divine Spirit, soul of the Church, that acts in every age and those

mysterious and effective interventions of the Spirit are manifest in our time in a providential way. The Movements and New Communities are like an outpouring of the Holy Spirit in the Church and in contemporary society. We can, therefore, rightly say that one of the positive elements and aspects of the Community of the Catholic Charismatic Renewal is precisely their emphasis on the charisms or gifts of the Holy Spirit and their merit lies in having recalled their topicality (relevance) in the Church.[3]

At the original Pentecost, believers are sent all over the globe to tell the message of the Second Coming and the approaching nuptial marriage. This new humanism that St. John Paul II sought, and his legacy still seeks, calls for a compelling dialogue: Who is the human person? St. John Paul II's Christian Humanism restores that New Pentecost in which we become once again temples of the Holy Spirit glorifying God in our body, allowing the Spirit to instill new and old charisms to re-evangelize the world.

LIVING THE NEW EVANGELIZATION

St. John Paul II's love for the New Evangelization is seen in his close collaboration with well-known evangelist Terry Law.[4]

Terry Law, an Oklahoma Evangelist, created a team of "Muscianaries" deemed Living Sound. Terry as lead member of this charismatic band powerfully preached the Gospel through the sound of music. Cardinal Stefan Wyszenski along with Cardinal Karol Woytyla, realized the power of God's presence working through Terry and so opened up their churches and cathedrals in 1974.

Terry impressed then Cardinal Karol Wojtyla when he was in Krakow performing because a young American woman studying abroad as an exchange student told the Polish Communist Party that they should invite Terry and his group to perform for the youth of Poland. Little did the Communist Party know Terry Law was an evangelist who studied at Oral Roberts University and graduated Summa cum Laude in 1969. His band performed and attracted the youth of the Poland because their unique ability to preach the Word through music. It was a gift, a charismatic gift in which God infuses himself into a person, in this case the members of the band, to touch the hearts, even those most hardened.

3. Benedict XVI, "Catholic Fraternity."

4. Interview with author James Gilbert, July 8, 2021.

Charismatic grace supernaturally infuses abilities beyond the natural talents. Music, one of the charismatic gifts, powerfully speaks to the hearts and souls of people, believer and non-believers alike.

Music speaks. It sweetly sings to the soul touching the core of our emotions. Tragedy or ecstasy; the misery or happy, the sensual or spiritual, music pierces and penetrates deeply and our hearts enter the mystery of the sound expressing what no painter, writer, or poet can. A form of beauty, musicians express the pathos of God touching the hearts of its hearers.

A talented musician, Terry had this gift for his music. His ability to connect his music with his charism distinctly displayed God's written Word in performances that supernatural touched people. How do we know this is true? The signs of charismatic graces are written through this unique story.

Charismatic graces are not for self-aggrandizement, but for selfless service that successfully moves others that otherwise would be impossible. Charisms of the Holy Spirit come from God; they are supernaturally empowered to do something great, beyond the ordinary. Finally, charisms have a courage and counsel that confronts and changes the outcomes.

Terry had this supernatural gift of music. The young woman experienced it and she, by the grace of God, influenced the Communist Party to invite this Christian band, Living Sound, to perform at a communist sponsored club in Krakow. During his first two performances, while the students were drinking and carousing, Terry saw the great spiritual need of these young college students, most of whom were studying English at university. Seeing their emptiness caused by atheism, Terry stopped playing and started preaching.

The young people received his gospel message with such enthusiasm that the club managers took him to the club basement for questioning, thereafter banning him from the platform during the band's second sell-out concert. But the songs were as powerful in their impact as any sermon. After the second concern, they garnered a long-standing ovation. The evangelizing went on all night long. Living Sound Team Members prayed with dozens of young men and women looking for meaning in their lives. The sensuality of the music awakened their spirituality. They wanted God!

When Terry received the invitation, he immediately said yes, not knowing that the Communist Party invited him and not a Christian group. Obviously, the incongruity creates a paradox that only can be understood through the working of the Holy Spirit. Two years after their first concert, both Cardinal Stefan Wyszenski and Cardinal Karol Wojtyla opened the nation's cathedrals and church to this group. St. John Paul II saw Terry's courage and capabilities to sing the scriptures, so the young people became awakened to the Spirit speaking to their hearts.

Preaching God in communist Poland created danger as the Communist strictly enforced their no God policy. Yet, Terry preached God. St. John Paul II had been preaching God for years. Now that the two met, they worked together to sing, pray, and prepare the hearts of hearers to open up to the inspiration of the Holy Spirit. Because of this encounter, Terry and St. John Paul II became such good friends that in 1980 now Pope John Paul II invited Terry to come and perform at a Wednesday Audience.

Music rooted in Gregorian Chant gives voice to our prayer filled with emotions, feelings, and sentiments. It unites. It harmonizes. It combines words and sounds moving the soul towards the divine. It expresses the power of our spirit when we cannot express the mysterious depths of the emotions we experience. It celebrates life and music reveals the movements we have in life from birth to death, sickness to health, sadness to joy, hate to love, divorce to marriage, loss to gain.

Terry gave his gift away; and because he gave, St. John Paul II and the rest of the world received this Pentecost, the fresh breath of the Spirit breathing new life into communist Poland and then to the rest of the world through St. John Paul II's confirmation.

KENOSIS: SELF-EMPTYING

> Jesus, who, though he was in the form of God, did not count equality with God a thing to be grasped, but emptied himself, by taking the form of a servant, being born in the likeness of men. (Phil 2:5–7)

The transcendence we desire comes through kenosis, the self-emptying of all that is unworthy of God. As Christ emptied himself of all his glory and splendor upon the Cross plummeting into the depths of hell itself—the crucifixion—Jesus unites himself with our condition, sinful and suffering, only to be lifted up, not on a cross of death, but on the cross that heals. St. John Paul encapsulates this understanding as he writes,

> From the bright horizon of divine transcendence, the Son of God crossed the infinite distance between Creator and creature. He did not grasp on, as if to a prey, to his "equality with God", which was

due to him by nature and not from usurpation. He did not want to claim jealously this prerogative as a treasure, nor use it for his own interests. Rather, Christ "emptied", "humbled" himself and appeared poor, weak, destined for the shameful death of crucifixion; it is precisely from this extreme humiliation that the great movement of ascension takes off, described in the second part of the Pauline hymn (cf. Phil 2, 9–11).[5]

In this mature stage of theosis, we too empty ourselves of our own egoism, the ego-drama. Here without pride, envy, and rebellion, we open ourselves to the theo-drama. Focusing on God's passion, we too rise. His humility and meekness lift us into the divine presence. This takes place when we like Christ humble ourselves, becoming meek taking upon ourselves the yoke of our personal crosses. This is the secret ladder that St. John of the Cross describes. We must descend down the ladder from our egoism only to ascend the ladder when humbled and docile, we see Christ standing calling us, "Come and See" (John 1:39).

How do we embrace kenosis into our souls? We empty ourselves of that which brings us complacency and mediocrity, our personal idols and earthly expectations. As we allow the Spirit to remove these from, we find a new depth, a profound sense of wonder and awe that we are indeed alive and vibrant in the Spirit. He creates a secret animation which flows into us, entrancing us with the beauty of others and their charisms (1 Pet 4:10–11). We see the power of the faithful, building up the Body of Christ, helping the least of these of our brethren, so all may praise God. In short, we perceive and discern God's actions working to build the Kingdom of God within us, around us, and in the Church.

What is the price of this new sense of glory? Our complete self-emptying. St. John of the Cross unveils for us the mystery of kenosis: "All the delights and satisfactions of the will in the things of the world compared to all the delights that is God are intense suffering, torment, and bitterness."[6]

In the paradox of kenosis, God empties us of our self-centeredness in order to pour his life-giving Spirit into us. This is the mature stage of theosis, called kenosis. "For you know the grace of our Lord Jesus Christ, that though he was rich, yet for your sake he became poor, so that you by his poverty might become rich" (2 Cor 8:9). God alone initiates and fulfills our indwelling of the inscrutable *Communio Personarum*.

---

5. John Paul II, "General Audience, November 19, 2003."

6. John of the Cross, *Ascent*, 1.4, 7.

Through kenosis, we climb the summit of the spiritual life. Ascending, God fully renews his image within us, as we seek to see through the window of faith the Face of the Father.

Kenosis begins with repentance and submission; even surrender. We cannot root sin out of our souls; we allow Divine Beauty to break the bonds of sin and so doing, he purifies us. Yet, this purification process will be painful—very painful—but cathartic! When the hand of God grabs the very source of our sin and begins to tear them out of our soul, we suffer immensely. Yet, this very act of tearing us free of the source of our sin—the ego-drama—reveals to us the immeasurable suffering that Christ endured on the cross.

Only in suffering do we understand transcendent grace for when we suffer, we count it all joy—even rejoice in our sufferings—for we know that when we unite our sufferings to Christ's sufferings out of love, he is transforming us, restoring us into full *communio*.

On our quest, we understand the greatest insight of scripture: that Jesus Christ comes to reconcile our fallen nature, heal us from the Fall, and restores us as sons and daughters animated by the Spirit.

> Christ goes toward His own suffering, aware of its saving power;
> He goes forward in obedience to the Father, but primarily He is
> united to the Father in this love with which He has loved the world
> and man in the world. And for this reason St. Paul will write of
> Christ: "He loved me and gave himself for me."[7]

The Incarnate Word in his Passion gives us holy and life-giving water flowing from his side, flooding our being with meaning, purpose, and understanding. But to receive this life-giving force—the Blood of Christ—and this soul cleansing water—the Spirit of Christ—both flowing from the side of the Crucified One, we submit, not to be dominated by the power of the Almighty One, but to be empowered as he comes and places himself beneath us to raise us.

In the growing union of kenosis, he kisses me with the kisses of his lips, and moves us into a new relationship with God which we now know as theosis. His Soul becomes my soul and my soul belongs to his Soul.

The Incarnation of Jesus infuses divine beauty into us through this grace: this kiss of the Holy Spirit. He replicates his Divine Beauty in us. We have the indwelling of the Holy Spirit. The risen Lord absolutely displays

---

7. John Paul II, *Salvifici*, sec. 16.

the Glory of God and his divine beauty inspires us to be infused with his Divine Life as St. Paul VI reflects.

> More than once we have asked ourselves what the greatest needs of the Church are . . . what is the primary and ultimate need of our beloved and holy Church? We must say it with holy fear because as you know, this concerns the mystery of the Church, her life: this need is the Spirit . . . the Church needs her eternal Pentecost; she needs fire in her heart, words on her lips, a glance that is prophetic.[8]

Yet the Spirit requires absolute obedience, a holy discipleship, and wise docility. This too is the work of the Holy Spirit. Living in obedience, the Holy Spirit breathes perennial and powerful inspirations in our hearts, drawing us closer to the nuptial banquet.

In our theosis, Jesus promises a new Advocate who unveils for us the face of the Father. Jesus says, "He who has seen Me has seen the Father" (John 14:9). The Sermon on the Mount bares the fullness of the Father's heart as the Catholic Catechism explains: "The Beatitudes depict the countenance of Jesus Christ and portray his charity."[9]

Through kenosis, we no longer live in the dynamics of the Fall. We reject the temptation of being a god to ourself. We no longer try to prove our power over ourselves and others as did Eve. We experience both our subjectivity, a self-determining choice to dwell with Christ; and our objectivity as we befriend and live in God's Kingdom developing true friendships. In our self-determination, we choose to suffer with Christ. This is the objective reality. We must suffer. It is part of the human condition. Our sufferings, however deep and wounded they can be, ground us in the very Fatherhood of God. In suffering we entrust ourselves, and in trust, we live and move and have our being in the Trinity.

The human person must incorporate the personal encounter with God the Father, our private prayer, and the objective and historic movement of the Spirit working in the world into a dynamic whole subjective and objective. When our subjective prayer and objective work harmonize, Christ comes to unite us as his Bride, the Church. Broken, we are blessed and participate in divine life. St. Peter offers his insights here.

---

8. Paul VI, *Holy Spirit Animator.*

9. *Catechism*, sec. 1717.

Beloved, do not be surprised at the fiery trial when it comes upon you to test you, as though something strange were happening to you. But rejoice insofar as you share Christ's sufferings, that you may also rejoice and be glad when his glory is revealed. (1 Pet. 4:12)

As St. John Paul II says, only through suffering do we know transcendence. In rejecting our suffering, the sorrow happens that we are rejecting the Son of God who humbled himself to find us. Our sufferings and tribulations last only a moment, but the friendship and glory of being God's adopted son or daughter lasts for an eternity. God will not let us be tempted beyond our strength. On this truth, we trust and indeed pray for an increase of our suffering so that the Kingdom may bear fruit through our less than perfect efforts. Yet, Christ in his perfection allows us to participate in his sufferings, knowing that together eternal fruit is born through human endeavors.

In the fullness of the *Communio Personarum*, God re-creates the sinner with pure perfection. God delights in us and spends time with us so we may now enjoy his beauty and ours without the corruption of the Fall. Jesus, the Bridegroom, changes our natural human dignity into divine dignity once again. The incarnate Son of God clothes us with his radiance. Radiant beauty restores us did the Light of Creation, forgiven because of repentance, we cry, "As for me, I shall behold your face in righteousness; when I awake, I shall be satisfied with your likeness" (Ps 17:15). We become like him for we see him as he is (see 1 John 3:2).

KENOSIS'S PURPOSE: WAITING FOR THE BRIDEGROOM

Kenosis frees us; yet most people fear it for it demands a true sacrifice of self. Our Bridegroom who has a passion to fulfill our deepest desires asks that we trust him completely. Kenosis, sacrificing our self, carries us to our God-given destiny. Yet many fear for it truly is the unknown. But kenosis acts out of love and when we act from love—the very nature of who we are in God—we conquer all fears.

In kenosis, we live and seek our destiny. We are made for God and we seek the Face of God the Father. "Thy Face, O Lord, Do I seek" (Ps 27:8). This passage fulfills the anagogy: our ascent up the Mount to the Beatific Vision. His presence penetrates our lives deeply, transforming our heart,

mind, soul, and body. Kenosis opens our eyes to seek his Face and transformed he is our only joy.

We wait and watch for the Lord, like the ten virgins waiting with
lamps (Matt 25:1–13). Some of them have prepared themselves by bringing oil with them. They are ready. Dwelling in pure hope, they watch and
wait. The other five virgins are empty, not just their lamps, but their very
souls. They were empty not because of their lack of desire but their lack of
preparation. Their focus was wanting. With kenosis, we watch expectantly
for Bridegroom to take us to the Wedding Banquet. Through kenosis, the
Bridegroom prepares us; when we open ourselves to doing his will. The five
virgins unprepared were not allowing the Bridegroom to prepare themselves with this precious oil, such as Jacob poured on his Rock signifying
Christ's arrival.

In our kenosis, God constantly anoints us, putting his salvific oil into
our heart and soul. We no longer seek our own satisfactions in the world,
but we glimpse in the quick flashes the actions of heaven. Our practice of
asceticism is a small price to pay for even a momentary understanding of
the Kingdom of Heaven. We in faith understand that in God's timing, the
Holy Spirit enlightens us as an oil-filled lamp. In his flashes and sparkles of
light, we behold the glory of God the Father.

> It is written (1 Corinthians 13:12): "We see now through a glass
> in a dark manner, but then face to face." Now that which is seen
> face to face is seen in its essence. Therefore God will be seen in His
> essence by the saints in heaven.[10]

On the Mount, Jesus preaches, calls us to see God as Father. This is
our destiny: to know God as Father we come to know why we are created,
where we are going, and why we are living. "Come, you who are blessed by
my Father, inherit the kingdom prepared for you from the foundation of
the world" (Matt 25:34). Our destiny is to inherit the Kingdom.

Our encounter with Jesus as we sit on the mountain side, listening,
meditating, praying leads us to contemplate the divine essence—eternal
truths of beauty—revealed in Jesus' words. This destiny leads us to his
beauty. Though we pause and enjoy the mystical encounter, now we have a
mission as did Jesus have his mission. Pope Benedict states this with clarity.

> There is nothing more beautiful than to know Him and to speak
> to others of our friendship with Him. The task of the shepherd,

---

10. Aquinas, *Summa Theologica*, Suppl.92.1.

the task of the fisher of men, can often seem wearisome. But it is beautiful and wonderful, because it is truly a service to joy, to God's joy which longs to break into the world.[11]

What does Christ's beauty do for us who wait for the Bridegroom? In its mystical power, our friendship with Divine Beauty brings forth the wonder and awe of the heart. So simple, so pure, so perfect, God's supernatural beauty captivates our soul so that everything else fades into figments and shadows. His Beauty destroys despair for it creates life and life brings forth joy which we cannot help but reveal to another.

> This world—they said—in which we live needs beauty in order not to sink into despair. Beauty, like truth, brings joy to the human heart and is that precious fruit which resists the erosion of time, which unites generations and enables them to be one in admiration![12]

Beauty, a ray of marvel and wonder, penetrates the very depths of our being. Overwhelmed, we know we are in the presence of absolute glory, power, and majesty: We experience the Divine something we cannot live without as Pope Benedict states:

> Man can live without science, he can live without bread, but without beauty he could no longer live, because there would no longer be anything to do to the world. The whole secret is here, the whole of history is here." The painter Georges Braque echoes this sentiment: "Art is meant to disturb, science reassures." Beauty pulls us up short, but in so doing it reminds us of our final destiny, it sets us back on our path, fills us with new hope, gives us the courage to live to the full the unique gift of life.[13]

ST. JOHN PAUL II ON SUFFERING

St. John Paul II honestly acknowledged his suffering in losing his family and describes Jesus as his new family. Jesus became his true brother and friend, and indeed the true brother of suffering humanity, sinful and rejected. Mary became his Totus Tuus: All is Yours, a devotion that was more than a simple recitation of the rosary. St. John Paul II abandons himself

11. Benedict XVI, *Mass.*
12. John Paul II, *Artists*, sec. 19.
13. Benedict XVI, "Artists."

into the motherly love of Mary. He entrusted himself into her care as Jesus entrusted St. John into Mary's care. "Behold your son, Karol." In pure compassion, our brother Jesus says the same words to us. "Mary, behold your child."

Seeking the Face of the Father makes us temples of holiness, intensifying our love of God. This desire for God's righteousness and justice, however, involves suffering and persecution. We are to become healers of those suffering as did Jesus, the suffering servant. This mystery of suffering, as St. John Paul II tells us, is divine wisdom—not human. Human wisdom sees suffering, as absurdity and foolishness. Yet St. John Paul II describes suffering.

> But the words of the Gospel about the woman who suffers when the time comes for her to give birth to her child, immediately afterwards express joy: it is "the joy that a child is born into the world". This joy too is referred to the Paschal Mystery, to the joy which is communicated to the Apostles on the day of Christ's Resurrection: "So you have sorrow now" (these words were said the day before the Passion); "but I will see you again and your hearts will rejoice, and no one will take your joy from you" (Jn 16:22–23).[14]

St. John Paul II contended with suffering and pure evil throughout his life. Yet, despair he did not; but turned to the mystic whom he admired, St. John of the Cross, a mystic who reveals how to handle suffering.

As a doctoral student, St. John Paul II went to Rome to study and his dissertation delved into these great mysteries of faith with which he struggled. Why so much pain and suffering in the world, in my life. Why am I so alone, without family, country, and even my Church?

In his study, he found faith not in intellectual assent, or a dogmatic understanding of God, but found faith to be a window into the Beatific Vision. These mystical insights strengthened St. John Paul II, giving him depth to deal with his tribulations and trials.

Studying the works of St. John of the Cross, his counsel touched the heart and mind of young St. John Paul II who understood that the one who draws near to the Father when suffering, receives strength, enlightenment, and instruction. St. John of the Cross taught that the soul must be emptied of self in order to be filled with God. In this way, St. John Paul II's suffering did not derail his faith but purified it. He quoted John of the Cross on this.

---

14. John Paul II, *Mulieris Dignitatem*, sec. 19.

"Faith is increased by means of the active night 'by means of that emptiness and darkness and detachment from all things.'"[15]

The purified person becomes capable of a transformed intellect. St. John Paul II describes this. "It is only through the reception of a supernatural power that the cognitive faculty is supernaturally activated. In other words, once the intellect is disposed supernaturally by a divine infusion, it is capable of receiving divine truths."[16]

With the reception of divine truths, the ascent to union with God becomes possible. St. John Paul II explains this through the ideas of St. John of the Cross.

> Every created thing is united to God by a natural union by the very reason of its being, and, depending on the perfection of its being, it will be more or less a vestige of God. But this vestigial likeness to God, this natural perfection, is not capable of a supernatural union with God; it cannot pass beyond the limits of the divine essence and penetrate the intimate life of divinity. No perfections of the natural order suffice to attain union with God, for they all lack that "essential likeness" which would enable them to ascend to the order of the divine. But the virtue of faith does possess the essential likeness and is therefore able to lead to union with God. This means that faith enters the confines of the supernatural order and touches divinity itself; and hence it is capable of contributing in some way to the participated transformation of the soul that is gradually and successfully effected through grace and love. The capacity to do this is rooted in the very nature of faith, from which evolves its unifying power.[17]

Hence, all who seek union with God must be emptied of self in order to enter the supernatural order. Humanity and especially Christianity walk the path of faith through suffering. As a person then, we must expect suffering and, at certain times of our lives, intense sufferings. These sufferings call us closer to Christ, for he comes as the Divine Physician who submits to our cries for help. He seeks to heal and free us from the cause of suffering.

St. John of the Cross teaches us divine wisdom in the Way of Nothing. This poetry cuts us free from our complacency and mediocrity.

Not to the easiest, but to the most difficult;

15. John Paul II, *Faith*, 133, quoting John of the Cross, *Ascent*, bk. II, ch. 24, no. 8.
16. John Paul II, *Faith*, 72.
17. John Paul II, *Faith*, 52–53.

Not to the most delightful, but to the harshest;
Not to the most gratifying, but to the less pleasant;
Not to what means rest, but to hard work; Not to most, but to the least;
Not to the highest and precious, but to the lowest and the most despised;
Not wanting something, but wanting nothing;
Not go about looking for the best of temporal things, but for the worst,
To desire to surrender everything for Christ.[18]

St. John of the Cross continues his counsels, so the soul detaches from the sensate and sensual world to enter into the Dark Night of the Senses. To be completely free from worldly distractions, the senses—human desires—must die and the thirst for theosis—Dios par Participation—begins.

To reach satisfaction in all, desire satisfaction in nothing.
To come to possess all, desire the possession of nothing.
To arrive at being all, desire to be nothing.
To come to the knowledge of all, desire the knowledge of nothing.
To come to enjoy what you have not, you must go by a way in which you enjoy not.
To come to the knowledge you have not, you must go by a way in which you know not.
To come to the possession you have not, you must go by a way in which you possess not.
To come to be what you are not, you must go by a way in which you are not.[19]

On the journey of theosis, the suffering servant possesses nothing but cries out for the Beatific Vision. As we carry our cross, the sign of physical and spiritual death, we cry for life, facing death in that most famous of prayer,

My God, my God, why have you forsaken me? Why are you so far from saving me, from the words of my groaning? O my God, I cry by day, but you do not answer, and by night, but I find no rest. (Ps 22:1–2)

In our sufferings, we search for an answer: we search for healing like the merchant seeking the pearl. Jesus does not merely hear our prayer. He unites himself with us. He purchases us through this abandonment. Our search for the divine pearl is reversed. It is not me seeking the Pearl—Jesus Christ—but he is seeking me, his pearl, to give me his Spirit—essence.

18. John of the Cross, *Ascent*, 1.13.6.
19. John of the Cross, *Ascent*, 1.3.11.

The Pearl of great price is not a grain of sand transformed by the sea. The pearl is a relationship—a friendship—that transforms me into someone of great value. This friendship is a mystical marriage, a participation in the cup of blessing, in which I become one with my beloved as he gave himself to me, inviting me to love as he loves. The Father who sent the Son is also well pleased with me as he was with his Son, for the Son and I love one another. He is completing in me what is lacking as I open my door to his knocking.

The mystical marriage completes the way of theosis for the Bridegroom knocks at my door inviting me to follow him, but where he goes no one knows, except his Spirit. Now we open the sails of our soul to the Spirit so we can catch the breath—the love—of God and be filled completely as was Mary.

A *LECTIO DIVINA* ON THEOLOGICAL PEARLS: THE BEATITUDES

"Again, the kingdom of heaven is like a merchant in search of fine pearls, who, on finding one pearl of great value, went and sold all that he had and bought it" (Matt 13:45).

I need the gift of faith, not a belief system, but the understanding that faith is a friendship that gives me meaning beyond the here and now. This is the truth of who I am and why I am. I am the pearl of greatest value in his eyes; and the truth is, only in divine participation do I see my worth which no sin or stain can destroy.

I am his divine child in relationship with a Divine Brother. Through faith, I believe in my purpose which transcends all earthly treasures. I was made to be forever in friendship with another, Jesus Christ who sends me his Spirit. His Spirit comes to me through others who are my friends in Christ and love me through the Spirit. These faithful friends, helpmates, are gifts of the Helper Spirit.

In my experience of divine participation, I admit my immense emptiness living divorced from the Helper Spirit. I am without union, so I mourn. I mourn that all the earthly pleasures and possessions that I crave will never satisfy my desire for a helpmate. I want more: to be more, have more, seek more. I want to be divine. The sadness occurs when my wants turn me into a god unto myself.

When I recognize my immeasurable desire to have and realize that this world cannot give what I need, I look. Yes, but I am not at peace. I look for peace and once again find it not in this world with all its beauty and majesty, but I find it in the One who creates me, the One who breathes divine life into me. Not the spirit of this world, but the Holy Spirit for he gives me peace, not as the world gives peace. Peace fulfills my hope for I have all that I need now, him the Helper, only waiting for fulfillment.

Finally, my need to be forever partaking of his divine nature, I look for perfect love. Yet, when I look for perfect love, I find that I cannot have a perfect love unless I, first, have perfect love within my heart, soul, and strength. I merely crave for something that I cannot have because I am not able to produce perfect love within. So I wrestle with self love, as did Jacob, because I cannot give what I do not have.

My love is impure, from its very source. My power to love is filled with selfishness, using others to gratify and satisfy my needs. I wrestle within for my mind reveals to me this perfect love exists, but not in me. My memory knows of this perfect love, lost in paradise. Now my will seeks the mystery of perfect love, a secret, hidden power within wanting to be opened, used, and satisfied.

Searching for my perfect love, I look for one whose heart is clean "Who does not lift up his soul to what is false and does not swear deceitfully" (Ps 24:4). So I pray "Create a clean heart in me O God and renew a right spirit within me" (Ps 51:10). This catharsis achieves the self-emptying of anything selfish. My heart is cleansed from within and purges itself of every false spirit; so, no taint of any sin exists; and no desire to any sin exists.

Now I see another way exists, a more excellent way. To be poor in spirit opens in me the gift of faith in which I befriend another for I see my own poverty of soul. I cannot do in my flesh what my spirit desires to do to my soul. I want an immortal kingdom where I feast on friendship knowing through faith I am loved.

Jesus Christ says, "Come and see" (John 1:39).

A PERSONAL REFLECTION: OBEDIENCE AND ANNIHILATION

It was Monday morning, a blossoming spring day. The sun was warm; Easter had just passed. Life was surging forth. Flowers pushing through the frosted ground, trees trying to bud and blossom preparing a fall harvest, the grass once dormant now a yellow green, farmers running planters across barren fields, and the sounds of children yelling, screaming, playing during morning recess. Sitting at my desk preparing my final lessons plans for the week, the phone rang.

At the same desk seven years earlier, I sat preparing my lessons for class and the phone rang. That day was September 11, 2001. In a matter of hours, the world was shattered, broken into pieces never to be put back together the same. During class that afternoon, the jet flew over: Airforce 1 flying over Offutt Air Force Base sixty miles from my school. Everyone heard the jet as school was somber and silent and the hum of the jets deafened the silence.

Every life has a defining event. Something happens, the pin is sheared, and the tension and balance of the spring explodes. The rupture fractures and what was is gone. December 22 was another day that the phone rang. I had to tell the family doctor that my dad had died. I could barely speak and so my sister took the phone. Yet this shearing in my life became my anchor.

For many, death is an anchor dropped into the abyss of hell; but for me, that anchor was cast up into heaven and the rope became my lifeline out of the depths of death into the Light of Christ. Trust in Christ, faith will cast the anchor up into heaven; doubt during death, casts the anchor into hell.

Jonah, the disobedient prophet, teaches us that even if we cast our anchor overboard as he cast himself into the raging sea, God, the Father sent the whale to swallow him up only to lift him up. So too with us, when despair swallows us we ought to look up and cast our cares upon the Lord; but as we drown in desolation, even then, Our Father casts us a life-line, pleading with us to clutch tightly this thread of hope to heist us into trust.

Fatherless at fourteen, I saw my family spiral down into the darkness. The home of a once lively family now became a tomb of darkness. Seeing the darkness, somehow, I saw a light. That light led me to look elsewhere for meaning and purpose in life. My brother and sisters were getting married, having children, and life was moving on. My mother started working and tried to put life back into a broken soul. But for me, it was out of sync. It did not make sense. Why do the same thing that devastated my life?

Through the death of my father, I saw that married with children was not for me. I was being called to follow a different path. A path that forsook brother, sister, father, mother, children, lands. Like the Rich Man whose possessions owned him, through the death of my father, I was called to dispossess everything and follow him.

> See, we have left everything and followed you. What then will we have?" Jesus said to them, "Truly, I say to you, in the new world, when the Son of Man will sit on his glorious throne, you who have followed me will also sit on twelve thrones, judging the twelve tribes of Israel. And everyone who has left houses or brothers or sisters or father or mother or children or lands, for my name's sake, will receive a hundredfold and will inherit eternal life. But many who are first will be last, and the last first." (Matt 19:27–30)

God was calling me as he called the Rich Young Man. I wanted something other. What that other life was I did not know until that December day when I bought a bus ticket to Gallup, New Mexico. I spent 6 months on the Jicarilla Reservation teaching at the Catholic School there. In the solitude and silence, I prayed. I entered the presence of a living, loving Father, Whom I did not know well. But he spoke, I too like Jacob was chosen, calling me to come and follow so I would know not only the Father, but his Son and his Holy Spirit who inspired me through the death of my dad to seek another way; His Way, the way of truth, beauty, and goodness. This Way conquered death and gave life—eternal life. I left Dulce, New Mexico, changed; and by October that same year I bought another ticket, this time to Rome.

Having graduated from Marquette in 1984 with a degree in philosophy, I entered another university started in 1222 by the great masters of the Dominican Order, the greatest being St. Thomas Aquinas. This university affectionately called the Angelicum, because St. Thomas Aquinas was the angelic doctor of the Catholic Church who taught with such insights that his contemporaries thought he was angelic. The proper name of the university is Pontifical University of St. Thomas Aquinas in the City. Here I would embark on my life, an adventure that was anything but audacious.

Siting at the feet of the masters, teaching me the thought of St. Thomas and the Way of Jesus Christ, I was being trained to become a master myself. Learning is passive; teaching is active. Only through teaching does one begin to understand the lessons learned sitting at the feet of the Master.

My career was teaching for fifteen years, but the phone rang that spring morning. "Hello," I said. "Hello," the voice responded. "This is the bishop. I want you to move Your new assignment will be made public in a few weeks. You have 6 weeks to move." "Yes, bishop," I responded.

In thirty-five seconds, a chapter of my life ended, and a new chapter was about to be written. Why did I have to close this chapter and begin a new? Not because of my will but his will. Obedience is the hardest virtue to cultivate for it demands submission to another's will. The priesthood and the vows taken: chastity, prayerfulness, and obedience (religious take vows of chastity, poverty, and obedience) demand complete abandonment of will into the desires of another. This is the greatest challenge for any person, "Not my will, but yours, be done" (Luke 22:42).

Obedience is a lesson not learned sitting in a classroom, but understood only through suffering: living, navigating the changing currents, most of which we have no control over. You cannot have love without obedience, and you cannot have obedience without love.

Obedience, the abandonment into Divine Providence, annihilates our stubborn hearts. Through the devastating disasters that come dramatically changing the course of our lives are meant not to destroy our lives, but to shape them not according to our ways, but his Way!

Whether it is a phone call simply ordering one to move into a new assignment, a disease that cuts to the heart, or a death-blow of a loved one, obedience does not fight, but submits. Submission places the self under another's will. Only through love does one freely submit for submission to another grinds away every edge and crevice until all that is left is pure love.

> The soul's union with and transformation in God that does not always exist, except when there is likeness of love. . . . The supernatural union exists when God's will and the soul's are in conformity, so that nothing in the one is repugnant to the other. When the soul rids itself completely of what is repugnant and unconformed to the divine will, it rests transformed in God through love.[20]

As we submit, transformation takes place. It is not I who am under the weight of obedience, but obedience supports my weight.

---

20. John of the Cross, *Dark Night*, 2.5.3.

Chapter Eight

THE FIFTH STEP
The Marian Way

Mary always intercedes for us, opening the pathways, the Secret Ladder as John of the Cross called this. In her openness to holiness, she was overshadowed by the Holy Spirit, a gift we too can receive. Mary, as spouse of the Holy Spirit, becomes the new creation we all desire. We yearn to belong to God, not merely as an acquaintance but as a truly trusted and welcomed companion. We want to be embraced. The Holy Spirit embraced Mary, overshadowing and redeeming her, and in so doing she becomes the cause of our salvation, introducing her love into us.

St. Maximillian Kolbe expounds this saying that at the Annunciation Mary was asked to be the Spouse of the Holy Spirit. St. Maximillian defines for all those questioning Mary's role in salvation history that she is the created complement of the Trinity.

> In virtue of this spousal union formally denoted by the title Complement, Mary is able to enter as no other into the order of the hypostatic union, her soul being wholly divinized, because by the grace of the Immaculate Conception it has been 'transubstantiated' into the Holy Spirit.[1]

In her yes to this question, she becomes the mother of Jesus and she also nurtures divine life in us too. In her participation, she nurtures grace

1. Quoted in Fehlner, *Martyr of Charity*, 100–101.

and we become like her, full of grace. She received this freely and wants to give this to us freely.

St. Maximillian describes her as the Spouse of the Holy Spirit. The Holy Spirit is the Uncreated Immaculate Conception, while Mary is the Created Immaculate Conception. In the Annunciation, the Uncreated Immaculate Conception (Holy Spirit) encountered the Created Immaculate Conception (Mary). This union recreates and mirrors our original relationship when God was one with his creation, Adam and Eve. The fruit of this union is Jesus Christ, the Son of God and the son of Mary. In her perfected state, she leads us to the secrets of that ladder, the cross. Through the cross we too find transcendency.

Mary as the Spouse of the Holy Spirit becomes the channel in which Christ comes to us and we go to Christ. With this open door to the Kingdom of Heaven, we too behold the Beatific Vision and the Face of God the Father. When we go with Mary to behold the Face of God the Father, we see Love passing between the Father and the Son through the Holy Spirit, and we participate in the *Communio Personarum*. This three-fold relationship of dwelling in the Trinity satisfies every dimension of our being.

St. Maximillian, a spiritual son of St. Francis of Assisi, conceived his idea of Mary as the spouse of the Holy Spirit for St. Francis taught this centuries previous. In his beautiful prayer, St. Francis praises Mary as Sancta Maria Virgo.

> You are unique among women in the world; you are the daughter and handmaid of the most high supreme King and Father of heaven; you are the mother of our most holy Lord Jesus Christ; you are the spouse of the Holy Spirit.[2]

Indeed, St. John Paul II confirms what the Second Vatican Council affirms. Mary has a powerful intercessory presence not only for those in the upper room, but for us here and now. "The Council expressly underscores her prayerful presence while waiting for the outpouring of the Paraclete: she prays, "imploring the gift of the Spirit."[3] At the Annunciation the Holy Spirit had descended upon her, "overshadowing" her and bringing about the Incarnation of the Word.[4] St. John Paul II writes, "Unlike those in the Upper Room who were waiting in fearful expectation, she, fully aware of

---

2. Francis of Assisi, "*Sancta Maria Virgo.*"

3. John Paul II, "General Audience, May 28, 1997," sec. 2.

4. Paul VI, *Lumen Gentium*, sec. 59.

the importance of her Son's promise to the disciples (cf. Jn 14:16), helped the community to be well disposed to the coming of the 'Paraclete.'"[5]

Before Pentecost and after the Ascension, what did Mary do? In the days and weeks following the resurrection, Mary prayed for the mighty and gracious actions of God. She interceded, loved, and helped prepare us all to be overshadowed to receive the new life of the Pentecost, causing the Spirit of God to breathe once again over the chaos of fallen creation, restoring divine life upon all humanity.

In brief, when the fullness of time came for her to partake of the redemption of all creation, she repudiated Satan, while embracing her Redeemer, becoming as St. Irenaeus states, *Causa Salutis*, the cause of our salvation; or as some today purport, Mary is the co-redemptrix. That is, she unites herself to her Son totally and freely, giving her body as the Arc of the Covenant, so God may once again dwell with his people.

This unlocks the mystery of theosis as explained by the Church's Kerygma. Christ comes to restore—recapture—those captured in the snares of the Evil One and invites us to participate in his restoration as faithful stewards of his gifts given. Mary fulfills this kerygma of Christianity perfectly as she responds to the invitation to conceive of the Spirit and fulfill the Plan of Redemption of fallen humanity. At her Annunciation, she becomes the Spouse of the Holy Spirit. She is the Woman of the Proto-evangelium, crowned as the queen mother in the book of Revelation (Rev 12:1–6).

By her actions, she conveys the kerygma to us that God seeks to dwell with us and desires intimacy with us as originally designed.

> Behold, the dwelling place of God is with man. He will dwell with them, and they will be his people, and God himself will be with them as their God. (Rev 21:3)

In this restoration, we see the strength of God revealed by the presence of Gabriel—God is my strength—for God has the power and plan to restore his creation and take it back from the one who stole it from him. God does this by gifting new life into fallen humanity offering himself as the absolute gift of sacrificial love.

> Through her response of faith Mary exercises her free will and thus fully shares with her personal and feminine "I" in the event of

---

5. John Paul II, "General Audience, May 28, 1997," sec. 2.

the Incarnation. All of God's action in human history at all times respects the free will of the human "I".[6]

Each one of us is endowed with the personal I. We all have God's free will dwelling within for we are created in the *imago dei*. Yet we cannot re-create on our own, but with his divine power, we co-create. What we create is both material and spiritual. We too are artisans creating works of art from the elements of the earth. We also create life—human life—for we are made from love for love and love brings forth new love and life. We then reflect as created images the Uncreated *Communio Personarum:* a relationship of love.

Imaging Christ, when we choose—respond—as did Mary to conceive Christ's will in our lives, we too become co-redeemers for redemption is only understood through participation in God's divine plan of redemption. God dwells within us and we within him. In contemplation, we ponder, as Mary pondered. We study, meditate, reflect on the sacredness that sets us apart. Separated from the darkness of sin and death, we can contemplate him; and in so doing, he abides in us as he physically dwelt in Mary and she abided in her Son. St. Augustine profoundly reveals this our destiny in his Advent meditation.

> God who is faithful, put himself in our debt, not by receiving anything but by promising so much. . . . He promised eternal salvation, everlasting happiness with the angels, an immortal inheritance, endless glory, the joyful vision of his face, his holy dwelling in heaven, and after the resurrection from the dead no further fear of dying. This is as it were his final promise, the goal of all our striving. When we reach it, we shall ask for nothing more.[7]

We, as Mary, come to understand that the way to redemption is through suffering—not avoiding it. We too choose to suffer. United to Christ through our suffering, the Holy Spirit fills us as it filled Mary and being filled, the Spirit adopts us into the *Communio Personarum*. We behold—understand—the beauty of the Cross: Meditating on the cross and taking up our own cross, we are forgiven, freed, and restored through Christ's passion.

At Pentecost, the Holy Spirit comes as Tongues of Fire. Purified, we too become pure chalices filled to the brim with gifts, fruits, and charisms

6. John Paul II, *Mulieribus Dignitatem*, sec. 4.

7. Augustine, *Psalm 109, 2, Commentary on Psalms*.

through which we change the face of the earth, as Pope Benedict XVI witnesses:

> Dear friends of Renewal in the Holy Spirit, do not grow weary of turning to Heaven: the world stands in need of prayer. It needs men and women who feel the attraction of Heaven in their life, who make praise to the Lord a new way of life. And may you be joyful Christians! I entrust you all to Mary Most Holy, present in the Upper Room at the event of Pentecost. Persevere with her in prayer, walk guided by the light of the living Holy Spirit, proclaiming the Good News of Christ.[8]

Because of Mary's response becoming the fullness of the fruit of restoration, we, too, her sons and daughters standing with her at the foot of cross, behold the Beatific Vision, the New Jerusalem.

> After this I looked, and behold, a great multitude that no one could number, from every nation, from all tribes and peoples and languages, standing before the throne and before the Lamb, clothed in white robes, with palm branches in their hands, and crying out with a loud voice, "Salvation belongs to our God who sits on the throne, and to the Lamb!" (Rev 7:9)

Mary becomes the mother of all the living, for she became the mother of the One who restores life and Jesus becomes the new Adam, High Priest and King ruling over us through sacrificial love. They fulfill what the Protoevangelium promised, as St. Augustine describes. God "has promised men divinity, mortals immortality, sinners justification, the poor a rising to glory."[9]

MARY'S MISSION AS THE MERCIFUL EVE

As the spouse of the Holy Spirit, Mary is the pure evangelization bringing the Good News of her Son to the world and the world coming to her. Mary went to the hill country of Judah. She traveled to Bethlehem, the City of David. The Magi came to her. She went to Egypt, Nazareth, Jerusalem and traveled all of Israel with her Son in his mission. Mary is the merciful mother, evangelizing all while accompanying her Son.

---

8. Benedict XVI, "Renewal in the Holy Spirit."
9. Augustine, *Psalms 109.*

The power of the Holy Spirit sends her on mission as his spouse so we too will follow this Marian Way doing great things for God. Mary's greatness does not come from power, and certainly not pride. Because of her humility, Satan's skull is crushed. She teaches us humility too if we are going to crush sin and death from our lives. We too need to imitate her allowing God to pierce our hearts with that same sword as pierced her heart. Her yes sent her on mission evangelizing all of Israel. This missionary spirit inspires our yes too. We too humbly say yes and are to evangelize as she did.

We see her evangelical role as Mother of the Church as St. John Paul II quotes proclaims.

> We believe that the Most Holy Mother of God, the new Eve, the Mother of the Church, carries on in heaven her maternal role with regard to the members of Christ, cooperating in the birth and development of divine life in the souls of the redeemed.[10]

Mary actively develops our theosis as she develops divine life within our soul. Mary had the grace of the Holy Spirit pouring into her, begetting a wholly new creation, and in her gracious mercy, she does the same for us. Having endured the rigors of kenosis, Mary views our newly opened interior life, touching them with her maternal hand, comforting, consoling, challenging, and sending us forth to continue her holy work: bringing all souls to Christ.

When we listen to Mary, her yes inspires our yes. Saying yes, we open ourselves to theosis and become closer to her Son. She distributes into our soul both charismatic and sanctifying gifts. She nurtures them, opening our closed hearts through her motherly love.

Mary's yes is still resounding in the universe with both its original and dynamic power, because she intercedes bringing a new life in Christ. At the Annunciation, the Angel Gabriel calls her Full of Grace, a title of perfection and union with the Divine. St. Pius IX affirms this mysterious encounter which prepares Mary to be called not only Mother of the of the Church, Co-Redemptrix, Mediatrix of Grace, Cause of our Salvation, New Eve but also the Spouse of the Holy Spirit, created without that stain of Original Sin because of the prevenient grace received at the conception of her Son. Pope Pius IX explains this great mystery.

> Concerning the most Blessed Virgin Mary, Mother of God, ancient indeed is that devotion of the faithful based on the belief that

10. John Paul II, *Redemptoris Mater*, sec. 118.

her soul, in the first instant of its creation and in the first instant of the soul's infusion into the body, was, by a special grace and privilege of God, in view of the merits of Jesus Christ, her Son and the Redeemer of the human race, preserved free from all stain of Original Sin. And in this sense have the faithful ever solemnized and celebrated the Feast of the Conception.[11]

As the Immaculate Conception, Mary shares her purity with suffering humanity. Through her intercession, grace divinizes us. We are made whole as she was. This is the new reality of humanity: To bring restoration and divinization to all of creation is the New Evangelization.

St. John Paul II in his declaration of Mary as Totus Tuus understood her as a bridge to the fulfillment we all long for in this theosis: Divine Participation. Mary's generous and long-awaited response to Gabriel grounds the New Evangelization: we are called to go on mission and proclaim Christ through our servanthood as Mary did, as did St. John Paul II.

In her new motherhood in the Spirit, Mary embraces each and every one in the Church, and embraces each and every one through the Church. In this sense, Mary, Mother of the Church, is also the Church's model. Indeed, as Paul VI hopes and asks, the Church must draw "from the Virgin Mother of God the most authentic form of perfect imitation of Christ. . . . As Christians raise their eyes with faith to Mary in the course of their earthly pilgrimage, they "strive to increase in holiness." Mary, the exalted Daughter of Sion, helps all her children, wherever they may and whatever their condition, to find in Christ the path to the Father's house.[12]

THE FIRST SATURDAY

"You are God's own people, that you may declare the wonderful deeds of him who called you out of darkness into his marvelous light" (1 Pet 2:9): a people of life and for life.[13]

It was a dark Saturday, the first one of February 1989. Rome is a dingy gray this time of year, drizzly, damp, and dark. Tourism is at a low and most of the Italians settle down early in the evening. Yet, being the first Saturday of the month, devout Catholics recall the words of our Lady of Fatima. "I

11. Pius IX, *Ineffabilis Deus*, sec. 7.

12. John Paul II, *Redemptoris Mater*, sec. 47.

13. John Paul II, *Evangelium Vitae*, sec. 78.

want you to come here on the thirteenth of next month, to pray the rosary every day, and to learn to read. I shall later say what I want."[14] This was June 13, 1917 and ever since then people have been praying the rosary on the First Saturdays of the Month as Our Lady of Fatima asks. It was on July 13, 1917, that the Lady of Fatima also asked that we receive Holy Communion on that day in reparation for sin. What sins? It was in 1930, St. Lucia had another vision. This time it was Jesus himself who told her why he wanted good-will people to pray the rosary and receive Holy Communion on the first Saturdays of the month:

> There are five ways that people offend and blaspheme against the Immaculate Heart of Mary:
>
> 1. Offenses or blasphemies against the Immaculate Conception—its denial and/or ridicule
>
> 2. Against her perpetual virginity
>
> 3. Against her divine maternity, refusing to accept her as the Mother of God and mother of all mankind
>
> 4. Those who implant in children's hearts, indifference, contempt and even hate against our Immaculate Mother
>
> 5. Insults directed against her sacred images, displays of indifference or ridicule, and the infliction of damage to them.
>
> Hence, with the intention of making reparation to the Immaculate Heart for these five offenses, we are asked to:
>
> 1. Go to confession (Can be within eight days before or after the First Saturday)
>
> 2. Receive Holy Communion
>
> 3. Pray five decades of the Rosary
>
> 4. Keep Our Lady company for fifteen minutes while meditating on the mysteries of the Rosary.[15]

Marian devotion reveals it roots going back to the beginning: Adam and Eve. Adam is the created son of God. Jesus is the uncreated Son of God. Mary is the created Immaculate Conception, while the Holy Spirit is the Uncreated Immaculate Conception. As the Holy Spirit is the completion of the Holy Trinity in that he is the essence of Divine Love: the binding love between the Father and Son. Mary is also the completion of the Father's

---

14. EWTN, "Our Lady of Fatima."

15. EWTN, "Our Lady of Fatima."

love for his creation for she is the created spouse of the Holy Spirit interceding for us always.

St. Maximillian Kolbe, the martyr of Auschwitz, and Polish contemporary of St. John Paul II writes concerning Mary, she "inserted into the love of the Most Holy Trinity becomes, from the first moment of her existence, always, and forever, the Complement of the Most Holy Trinity."[16]

My mother had a deep Marian devotion. She prayed the rosary every evening and that night she wanted to go to the First Saturday devotion. We did. Arriving early, we chose to sit towards the back, on the right side in the hall. This was the best spot. Having lived in Rome long enough, I knew where to position myself and those with me so they would have the best chance to see him, meet him, and touch him.

The hemorrhaging woman in the Scriptures thought, "If I just touch his garment, I will be healed" (Matt 9:21). So too, many of the faithful just wanted to touch him, St. John Paul II, and be healed, inspired, and renewed. Listening to St. John Paul II recite the rosary, deep in meditation as 200 or so people gathered saying the rosary with him inspired me. The crowd afterwards pushed against the barriers, hands reaching, voices crying out in hope like the woman, they too hoped be healed of their pains.

I could not but think of this passage. Sheep lost looking for their shepherd and he was walking down the aisle, like a gauntlet of broken humanity each wanting to touch him, as though that touch would heal them. I saw this so many times at papal audiences and liturgies. People desperate as was the hemorrhaging woman and so many other stories in the scriptures, all wanting to touch Jesus—St. John Paul II—and receive an answer to their prayer.

As St. John Paul II came towards us, my mother was waving her hand with all the rest. I stood back letting the faithful come forward. Yet, he noticed me. Dressed in my cassock it was hard not to be noticeable. The crowd was more Italian and so many religious sisters and here I was taller than most, blonde, and in a cassock. He touched my mother's hand and then looked directly at me. Smiled, nodded his head, put out his hand towards me, and asked, "Are you English?"

Like Nathaniel, Jesus noticed, stopped, spoke to me. Nathaniel repented. He was renewed. This is accompaniment: To personalize and individualize. St. John Paul II identified me knowing, I must be a student, studying the rigors of theology. He reached out to me, knowing the meaning of the

16. Kolbe, *Scritti di Massimiliano Kolbe*, 1318.

slightest encouragement to a struggling student working through the complexities of theological training that challenges even the brightest of mind: my mind not so bright. His touch touched me knowing that he singled me out among the crowd to assure my discernment to my priestly vocation.

This scene repeated itself thousands of times as millions of people sought him for he was "Jesus" to so many. A few months earlier, I was chosen to be part of a group of Polish Patriots who came to Rome on pilgrimage. It was Wednesday and we planned to go to the papal audience in Paul VI Hall. Once again, knowing were to sit as they all wanted to see and touch St. John Paul II, we sat off to the side, the right side again as I knew he typically walked this way at the conclusion of the talk.

We sat, we listened, and everyone clapped and cheered when their name or group was called. So too this group cheered when they were recognized. The woman sitting next to me was older, obviously in anguish. She looked into my eyes at the conclusion of the talk, and I understood she wanted to touch her "Jesus."

I led her to the barrier though we were several layers behind the crowd. As St. John Paul II came closer, she reached out and started yelling. I pushed her forward and when St. John Paul II heard her, he looked at her. His face was distressed. He reached out his hand specifically to touch hers, but they could not reach. I pushed a bit more and their hands touched. She was visibly shaken. Emotions flooded her face. Tears, whether of sadness or joy, I could not tell, but I had to hold her up and help her out of the hall.

I do not know what she said or why St. John Paul II looked at her directly and made the effort to touch her specifically. But like the woman believing that a touch would heal her, so too this woman believed, as I witnessed, his touch overwhelmed her.

This too is accompaniment. Personalizing a person and seeing them as a subject—not as an object—giving them that touch as did Jesus, as did St. John Paul II.

St. John Paul II reached millions and changed history, yet behind this power and thinking and writing and indeed, changing the political situation in Europe, stood Mary, interceding, consoling, giving wisdom, even correcting. Mary called St. John Paul II, calls all of us, to the perfection known through theosis.

SECTION THREE

Theosis: Desiring the Beauty of God

Chapter Nine

THE SIXTH STEP
The Nuptial Marriage

JOHN OF THE CROSS: THE FULFILLMENT OF THEOSIS

St. John Paul II lived the truths that John of the Cross reveal to us.

> In the inner wine cellar
> I drank of my beloved, and when I went abroad
> Through all this valley
> I no longer knew anything,
> And lost the herd which I was following.[1]

I am to be possessed by righteousness that is not mine but his who makes me righteous through the wine of his blood from his pierced heart. The shedding of his blood is the power of Love Divine. Everything that he is is mine and everything that I am is his. That is the essence of Covenantal Love: his life for mine and my life for his. He pours out love for he is Love himself; and as he freely gives to me, he is inviting me to be divinely possessed and not self-possessed.

---

1. John of the Cross, *The Spiritual Canticle*, stanza 17.

Divinely possessed, I am pure, denuded of all that is not love; and because I am transformed by his grace, I become one with him as bride to groom: the two of us becoming one, a *communio* of me with him.

Denuded and annihilated from my thirst for power, my lust for pleasure, and my greed for possessions, I enter theosis. I am in full communion, a physical and spiritual union, with my God, My Divine Confidant in Whom I entrust my heart, mind, and strength. Now I am a new creation in Christ, living the Law of the Gift which delivers me from using another for myself; but empowers me to give myself as he has given himself to me. Now I am a gift to be possessed by the other: the Bridegroom himself.

To be possessed by the Bridegroom is our marital exchange; and I, through the divine reflection of *Lectio Divina*, experience then embrace the mystery of love. I am the spouse Whom the Bridegroom desires with all his heart. I enter the Eucharistic wedding banquet, not as a guest, but as his bride. I fall in love with him for he is now my spouse. I exchange my human essence for his divine presence and he wants to fill me for he sees me as his own, the chalice of his love. He pours out his blood, pierced by hate only to bleed love divine. My chalice, as I watch and wait meditating on his passion of love, overflows, the wine of gladness fills my soul; and I drink deeply only to be anointed with the oil of gladness. Now my soul, a chalice of clay, brims over for I am completely transformed. He dwells in me and I dwell in him and where I am he is here and where he is, I am there.

Through reflection on the Story of my Salvation, I go beyond mere personal meditation and enter divinely infused contemplation. I see him with my interior eyes—the eyes of faith—and I behold I am the son, the daughter, of the Father who thought of me from all of eternity. Now is the day I see my eternity for I am full of grace. I have been prepared by my Father through the gift of his Son to enter into this mystical union in which I am clothed, not with garments of gold or a diadem of jewels, but with his Divine Wisdom, the sweet knowledge of righteous love.

> I will greatly rejoice in the Lord;
> my soul shall exult in my God,
> for he has clothed me with the garments of salvation;
> he has covered me with the robe of righteousness,
> as a bridegroom decks himself like a priest with a beautiful headdress,
> and as a bride adorns herself with her jewels. (Isa 61:10)

The Lord, my Bridegroom, completely possesses me and I, along with all of Israel old and new become the beloved spouse. This spousal intimacy, a relationship with Divinity, invites everyone who desires to be possessed by the Divine Bridegroom for he knocks at the door of every person, even the most desolate and hollow.

> You shall no more be termed Forsaken,
> and your land shall no more be termed Desolate,
> but you shall be called My Delight Is in Her,
> and your land Married;
> for the Lord delights in you,
> and your land shall be married.
> For as a young man marries a young woman,
> so shall your sons marry you,
> and as the bridegroom rejoices over the bride,
> so shall your God rejoice over you. (Isa 62:4–6)

I have a new identity now, through selflessness, a fruit of the Holy Spirit. Being inspired by his presence, I am a temple of the Holy Spirit. Theosis completes me. Fully and utterly, I partake openly in the fruits of docility and humility, being perfected in spiritual joy seeing the nuptial union of humanity with divinity.

Chapter Ten

THE SEVENTH STEP
Christian Perfection: Oneness

THE BEATIFIC VISION, THE divine *Communio Personarum*, like Abraham's
three visitors, calls to us from the edge of our consciousness.

> Behold, I stand at the door and knock. If anyone hears my voice
> and opens the door, I will come in to him and eat with him, and he
> with me. The one who conquers, I will grant him to sit with me on
> my throne, as I also conquered and sat down with my Father on
> his throne. He who has an ear, let him hear what the Spirit says to
> the churches. (Rev 3:20–21)

What stops our union with God and one another? The source of all
division is mediocrity, the source of union is humility. In our humanity, we
wrestle with the paradox and contradiction of these two forces: mediocrity
and humility, carried within our being.

> As for the spiritual faculties of man, this deterioration consists
> in the clouding of the capacity of the intellect to know the truth,
> and in the weakening of free will, which is weakened in the face
> of the attractions of sensitive goods and is more exposed to false
> images of the good elaborated by reason under the influence of
> the passions. But according to the teaching of the Church, it is a
> relative deterioration, not an absolute one, not intrinsic to human
> faculties. Therefore, even after original sin, man can know the fun-
> damental natural truths, even religious ones, and moral principles
> with his intellect. He can also do good works. We must therefore

speak rather of a darkening of the intellect and a weakening of the will, of "wounds" of the spiritual faculties as well as of the sensitive ones.[1]

On one hand, confusion fills our minds and we are clouded with ignorance; on the other hand, passion drives us toward perfection for we have a passion for excellence. In the clash of these truths, we sense the power of the Lamb to perfect us in preparation for our union in the Kingdom of God where all tribes, peoples, and languages offer the sacrifice of praise to the Lamb upon the Throne

Theosis powerfully implicates this paradox. We know not only our individual excellence but the perfection to which Christ calls all person to live in his kingdom, we know as his Church. Indeed, all Christians, united to Christ desire not only our own spiritual perfection, but the perfection of all so that all may be one in Christ.

> That we all may be one. As you, Father, are in me and I am in you, may they be in us so that the world may believe that you have sent me. (John 17: 21)

Jesus' Farewell Discourse culminates his earthly ministry convincing us with these authoritative words, that God calls all human beings to union not only with him but with each other. This directive is sheer grace making us one body, the Body of Christ. The Holy Spirit anoints us, being the bonding agent, and unites us intimately with the Trinity. We are ennobled with this grace because as the Father is in the Son and the Son is in the Father, we too are present with them, dwelling in their great love through the power and presence of the Holy Spirit whom Jesus promises to send us once he leaves. We are to live in the *communio personarum*, one with another, as we dwell in the *Communio Personarum* with God.

Yet this prayer also challenges our heart because of the gap between this ideal of unity and the reality of our disunity. Numerous and profound divisions exist in the body of Christ because we are not unified with each other, much less are we united with the Trinity if we are not united with each other. Our union with the Trinity overwhelms us because we so easily say and feel we love God fulfilling the command, but somehow hate our brother or sister.

> If anyone says, "I love God," and hates his brother, he is a liar; for he who does not love his brother whom he has seen cannot

1. John Paul II, "General Audience, October 8, 1986," sec. 7.

love God whom he has not seen. And this commandment we have from him: "whoever loves God must also love his brother." (1 John 4:20–21)

Satan, the demon who divides and creates a divorce between each other, sows suspicions through deceptions—the false promises that we will be happier if we are hateful. Within Christianity, Satan spreads discord concerning Jesus' prayer for unity as if this notion of oneness is nonsense. Yet Jesus' words are spoken from the fullness of his Godhead, in which he and the Father are One and the Spirit of their love binds them into the *Communio Personarum*. His words are not fairy-tale metaphors but divine commands: We are to love one another as he loves us!

How do we become one? Clarity emerges amidst the struggle when we endure and protect unity. In our clouded minds, we desire to become mortal enemies with each other. Yet Jesus clearly commands us in an earlier admonition from the Sermon on the Mount. "Be perfect, therefore, as your heavenly Father is perfect" (Matt 5:48). Perfection of person detaches us from our ways and wants so we may attach ourselves to God's ways and wants. Throughout his preaching, Jesus commands individuals differently because the Father has different purposes for each of us. Because God's will is unique for each person with a different calling, each person must detach themselves from their particular source of division as we see Jesus wisely counsel the rich young man, "If you wish to be perfect, go, sell your possessions, and give the money to the poor, and you will have treasure in heaven; then come, follow me" (Matt 19:21). As we know, the rich young man, rejecting Jesus' call to be perfect, went away divided, because his heart, attached to his possessions, separated him from his brother Jesus, although he recognized Jesus as his teacher and master, a man speaking the truth of God.

The origin for this directive for personal perfection comes from Leviticus 19:2, known as the earlier type or typology of divine wisdom. "The Lord spoke to Moses, saying, 'Speak to all the congregation of the people of Israel and say to them: You shall be holy, for I the Lord your God am holy.'" Jesus' teachings concerning personal perfection are nothing new. They encompass the teachings of the Old Testament, but the difference is this. Jesus has authority and power that cuts—circumcises the heart—making the student decide to either be a complete and committed disciple or merely a disciple of convenience and opportunity, as the rich young man was.

In all of his prayers, commands, and admonitions, Jesus' call for all believers to become holy and perfect, sacred in the eyes of the Lord, are not just for a few predestined ones. It is for all. Our Creator created us in perfection and after the Fall he seeks to recreate all of us perfectly which becomes realized in our personal and perfect union with God through our unique calling.

> Fortified by so many and such powerful means of salvation, all the faithful, whatever their condition or state, are called by the Lord, each in his own way, to that perfect holiness whereby the Father Himself is perfect.[2]

In these commands of oneness, Jesus outlines the way of theosis, personal perfection in which the Holy Spirit anoints us and we are divinized, brought into perfect union with the Father. "Be you perfect" becomes our life's call, to grow into union with God so we may love as the Lord loves us. Only in pure fearless love do we seek and then see the Face of our Father.

St. John Paul II describes the magnificent scope of God's passionate actions reaching out to save us.

> The Holy Spirit, already at work in the creation of the world and in the Old Covenant, reveals himself in the Incarnation and the Paschal Mystery of the Son of God, and in a way "bursts out" at Pentecost to extend the mission of Christ the Lord in time and space. The Spirit thus makes the Church a stream of new life that flows through the history of mankind.[3]

The Spirit bursts out at Pentecost, creating the church then and now. God still creates and pours the Spirit upon us, calling us to unite in our fulfilled theosis. God is always creating us, interceding for us, showing his passion for us, so we may experience him personally.

The continuing creation of the universe and Pentecost makes all things new: a New Pentecost unites us, a New Evangelization sends us out. In the heavenly realms, all divinely inspired actions continually reach out to raise fallen humanity: we may all through eyes of faith see angels ascending and descending upon the Son of Man.

In God's time, the Holy Spirit infuses his perfection into us as a gift: the self-donation of his very essence becomes our living, breathing, and empowering perfection. The beauty of God's perfection abiding in our

2. Paul VI, *Lumen Gentium*, sec. 11.

3. John Paul II, "Ecclesial Movements," sec. 4.

being makes us as luminous as a rare pearl, as brilliant as the perfect diamond. God's essence creates a living temple within our hearts, filled with the Shekinah, the glory of God. And after growing in the great gift of re-creation with its struggles, self-emptying, and even annihilation of self, we discover the truth "That we all may be one." For this command given to us by the living Son of God, causes oneness and unites us with God and with one another, if we participate and do what Jesus commands: sell anything and everything that detaches you from full participation in Me.

Even now still attached to our divisions, we participate in the Trinity, Father, Son, and Holy Spirit. In this great gift of participation, we join in union with other believers desiring "that we all may be one." Through our divine worship, the Sacred Sacraments, especially the new Passover Meal, we unite as the Body of Christ praying that we all be one; that is, we all be forgiven, we all become forgiving, and we all do the will of Father for he has called each of us by our name.

Theosis calls to us, offering spiritual completion. Jesus says, "Be perfect as your Father in heaven is perfect" (Matt 5:48), and in our obedient response going the way of theosis, we fulfill Jesus' fruitful prayer for oneness. Our humble offering in this book is to show what the Church Fathers, St. John Paul II, Pope Benedict, St. Paul VI, and the great mystics have shown us in their lives and their witness: Our lives are meant for theosis, the giving of ourselves, our being and souls, to God who in his gracious and generous mercy, accepts us, calls us, even loves us, uniting himself with us.

A PERSONAL REFLECTION NOME

The blue tail shrieked across the sky. The roar of the jet engines deafened my ears. Alaska Airlines flight 153 just took off and flew over the Church, St. Joseph's Church, Nome Alaska. An hour earlier that same jet dropped me off at the Nome Airport; and now in my new assignment as pastor, I watched it take off and fly away. It was my only ticket out: No roads lead to Nome.

Nome, Alaska. Home to one of the largest gold deposits in the world when three lucky Swedes Jafet Lindeberg, Erick Lindblom, and John Bruynsteson digging in the Anvil Creek found gold in 1899. Population of Nome that day was thirty. In 1900 over sixty thousand people came to this remote, isolated, and desolate fishing village seeking their fortune. Who could forget Wyatt Earp and Tex Rickard who came and built booming saloons leaving Nome all the richer. Raold Amundsen explorer the South Pole also famously came to Nome in 1906 after a three-year journey through the Northwest Passage. Home to Jimmy Doolittle the World War II hero who bombed Tokyo. Also, Alberta Schenck Adams, a native woman, defied the segregation laws. Her witness contributed to the 1945 Alaska Anti-Discrimination Act.

Home to the Iditarod which recalls the famous great race to get the diphtheria serum to Nome during the 1925 epidemic. The Last Train to Nowhere brought from New York City to the Solomon (Gold) River (just east of Nome) in the 1900s hoping to build a rail system on the Seward Peninsula. Now it sits sinking into the tundra rusting away. A major storm hit just a few years after the construction of the rail system which destroyed both the tracks and the dream to build a railway up the river of gold to carry down the deposits of gold to the port. A few days of wind, rain, and snow melted the permafrost. Tundra melts, moves, and no one builds on the shifting permafrost. It could never support a rail system. Like the River to Nowhere so now the Train to Nowhere, I did not know where I was; or why. But the Holy Spirit did!

Nome is the gateway to Bering Sea. Home to Anvil Mountain and the Dew Line: Distant Early Warning Line and Ballistic Missile Early Warning System used by the military until new systems were created in Clear, AK. Finally, the famous Board of Trade Building built on Front Street, the street which fronts the Bering Sea was the Sin-City Town Council and Saloon. The patrons made up the rules for the city daily.

Faithful Catholics arrived here early, and priest Fr. Aloysius Jacquet, SJ, was sent to Nome in 1901 to build a Catholic Church. He maniacally worked from July 1 to November to finish St. Joseph Catholic Church before winter set in. It was finished and he soon left.

Now, Old St. Joseph Catholic Church sits in the center square. It served as the Church for the Catholics in the area until 1944. Not built for arctic winters but more like a Gothic cathedral in the high plains of Nebraska, eventually it had to be replaced by another church much smaller. Then in 1994, a new modern church built for the arctic climate with eighteen inch walls and very few windows was constructed. It was home sweet Nome for eighteen months of my life.

As the jet left, the perfect blue sky looked black, a darkness came over me. Alone, isolated, deserted in this frozen wasteland, I asked, What am I doing? I left my peaceful assignment four weeks earlier driving up the famous Al-Can Highway built by the Core of Engineers during World War II to connect the lower 48 with the new military base the whole state of Alaska.

Our Lady of Sorrows Catholic Church set in the western high plains of Grant, Nebraska. Quaint and picturesque it was a throw-back to yesteryear. One could have been living there as though it was 100 years ago.

Grant is seventeen miles distant from Venango the last town in Nebraska, a Colorado border town. Here, the cowboys and cowgirls live. The rolling plains, sweeping grasslands, the hot dry summers and the brutal blizzards came rushing across the western plains, where the trade winds of the Pacific Ocean collide with the hot and humid currents of the Gulf of Mexico. These two weather systems battle as to which way the wind will blow and produce the most dramatic weather. And when the arctic winds of the north sweep down from the Bering Sea, a winter white out comes blinding the land with snow and ice. The scenery was made for a movie, but this was real life here in Grant with real men and women carving out a living in a western world.

It was a perfect, peaceful, priestly life ministering to the ranchers and farmers, dealing with families, friends, and the faith community. To me it was paradise. Yet, sitting in a clergy meeting, the bishop mentioned his friend, a new bishop of Alaska wanting missionaries: Go North to Alaska.

I heard: North to Alaska? Bishop Chad Zielinski invited anyone and everyone to come North. Become a missionary. Live the Alaskan dream. Seek adventure! Discover Gold! Hunt, fish, camp, hike! Ride the dog-sleds, canoe the Yukon, Go North "young" man—not West! Become a missionary as in the days of old: conquer the Last Frontier!

Nostalgia swept over me: The Call of the Wild, White Fang, the Klondike Trail. The extreme, the intense, it was on the edge of nowhere. Yet, here in the comfort of the seminary, sitting in our conference hall, perfectly content enjoying my quaint assignment, the Spirit spoke through that voice. Experience the extreme, the intense! Was I to see what was over the edge?

That first evening in Nome, I sat sitting in a small dining, living room waiting for the sun to set, I cried, "What have I done?" That first night, I sat in darkness under the light of the midnight sun.

In the darkness and silence, I experienced kenosis. I was empty, a nobody, living nowhere. I left my world to come to this world. Here, the voice of the Spirit began to speak. I listened: "Not your way but my way!" the voice spoke. I too would enter the darkness that St. John Paul II explained years earlier in Rome, defending his thesis, explaining that by the darkness of faith we participate in the light of God. St. John of the Cross describes this dark night.

> Faith, manifestly, is a dark night for souls, but in this way it gives them light. The more darkness it brings on them, the more light it sheds. For by blinding, it illumines them, according to those words of Isaiah that if you do not believe you will not understand; that is you will not have light (Isa 7:9).[4]

As St. John Paul II said, heart speaks to the heart, even from afar. History explores the lives and hearts of those who lived long ago, not to obtain facts and figures, dates and times, but to fill our hearts with the light of divine truth, often lost in earthly time, to renew our waning hearts.

> This human, first-hand and "historical" witness to Christ is linked to the witness of the Holy Spirit: "He will bear witness to me." In the witness of the Spirit of truth, the human testimony of the Apostles will find its strongest support. And subsequently it will also find therein the hidden foundation of its continuation among the generations of Christ's disciples and believers who succeed one another down through the ages.[5]

St. John Paul II gripped by the conviction that in destitution and desolation, the radical and beautiful light of truth, the Son of God comes

---

4. John of the Cross, *Ascent*, 2.3.4.

5. John Paul II, *Dominum et Vivificantum*, sec. 2.

seeking us with the very passion of a Father looking for his prodigal son. His passion looks for our heart, hoping that we open the door to the magnificent, heavenly realms brought to us by the simple presence of a humble man riding on a donkey. Living in this Light of Truth—the darkness of faith—is our only safety when living in the dark night. Loving this Truth, our Light, is our only glory. Savoring this Spirit of Truth, it is our only happiness. Yet, the Light of Truth blinds us from natural truths so we can experience the supernatural Truth: the Holy Spirit breathing divine life into our human hearts.

The Resurrected Lord commands, Go into the world making disciples of all nations, reminding us that he sends his Spirit so we may know: "Behold I am with you always even to the end of the age" (Matt 28:20). The New Pentecost comes when we live in darkness, blind to the world fallen in sin. In the darkness, the Risen Lord tells us, "Behold I make all things new!" (Rev 21:5). This is the new eternal Pentecost, ever present in our hearts if we have the eyes of faith. St. John Paul II had the eyes of faith; having been blinded by the destruction of his civilization, he saw history through faith—not sight—and called each believer, called me in the darkness of the midnight sun to go and make new disciples on the streets of Nome.

Chapter Eleven

THE EIGHTH STEP
Theosis: The Nuptial Marriage

IN DECEMBER 1979, ST. John Paul II in a private audience convincingly stated concerning the power of the New Pentecost.

> I am convinced that this movement is a sign of His action. . . . Now I see this movement, this activity everywhere. In my own country I have seen a special presence of the Holy Spirit. Through this action, the Holy Spirit comes to the human spirit, and from this moment we begin to live again, to find our very selves, to find our identity, our total humanity. Consequently, I am convinced that this movement is a very important component in the total renewal of the Church in this spiritual renewal of the Church.[1]

St. John Paul II stated that the Second Vatican Council brought forth spiritual fruits. To the Italian National Service Committee in April 1998, John Paul said the following.

> The Catholic charismatic movement is one of the many fruits of the Second Vatican Council, which, like a new Pentecost, led to an extraordinary flourishing in the Church's life of groups and movements particularly sensitive to the action of the Spirit. How can we not give thanks for the precious spiritual fruits that the Renewal has produced in the life of the Church and in the lives of so many people? How many lay faithful - men, women, young people,

1. John Paul II, *Private Audience*, 279.

133

adults and elderly - have been able to experience in their own lives the amazing power of the Spirit and his gifts! How many people have rediscovered faith, the joy of prayer, the power and beauty of the Word of God, translating all this into generous service in the Church's mission! How many lives have been profoundly changed! For all this today, together with you, I wish to praise and thank the Holy Spirit.[2]

St. John Paul II explains in his Christian humanism that we are made for God. We are perfectible by his Pentecost. This is the New Evangelization! The Spirit of God reveals that through his power to perfect, we become friends of the Living God and cannot help but preach this message to those looking for perfection in their lives. This evangelization restores our dignity through spiritual adoption—filiation—in which we belong, become one again with our Father, through the Son and Spirit.

It is not only the theological gifts of the Divine Artisan that I seek; but I seek the Giver himself. This perfect happiness satisfies for it does not come from the mind of man; it comes from the heart of the Redeemer and he is the fulfilment of all my desires.

The Christian Humanism called for by St. John Paul II directs our desire for a New Evangelization which calls upon the Holy Spirit to come anew and refresh and restore what was lost. In the Spirit, we look beyond the ugliness of humanity and the evil that causes it. The Pentecost delves deeply into our hearts transfiguring them, then transcending us from merely fallen beasts controlled by our passions, to become temples of the Spirit filled with his gifts, fruits, and charisms that make us divinely true, good, and beautiful. We are fully human and full of the divine: full of grace.

This is the New Pentecost, this is the New Evangelization that St. John Paul II outlined in 1959, giving the world a new humanism because the man-centered humanisms emptied all mankind of any personal identity, any self-value, of any identity outside the social and political structures of the state, and most tragically from any spiritual perfectibility. This New Pentecost begins with docility and humility: the ability to be discipled, giving us the spiritual skills to deal easily with the challenges of life (Prov 1:7), or as St. Teresa tells us:

---

2. John Paul II, "To Leaders Renewal in the Spirit," sec. 1.

For if at some time the Lord should grant us the grace of impress-
ing his love on our hearts, all will become easy for us and we shall
accomplish great things quickly and without effort.[3]

Though this grace, we have a personal and disciplined relationship
with both. We are a child loved by the Father and we are united to the
Father through our faithfulness to the Son, our Bridegroom who makes us
fruitful. Now, all my relationships with others: marriage, family, friends,
and even myself, are rightly ordered. They have mindfulness and heartful-
ness ordered unto truthfulness, goodness, and beauty.

In essence, the New Pentecost re-defines me as a person. I am not an
isolated individual without purpose, nihilism, or a social object made to
produce for the fatherland, socialism; but I am the *imago dei* of the Divine
Artisan. With a heart and mind docile to the Spirit, I allow divine love to
discipline me which perfects me.

Perfectibility is realized when I, like my Bridegroom, become a gift
to another. I am a person-gift, as Jesus was to us from the Father. I am
personally fulfilled and perfected as I donate myself to another out of pure,
unadulterated love. I become a person-gift first to God which allows me to
love another freely as Christ loved me. Christ the Bridegroom personal-
izes and perfects us as his bride in a nuptial marriage, the ultimate human
expression and experience of theosis.

The man, Adam, sacrificially donates himself to his bride Eve who
receives this gift and in return gifts her total self to Adam. In this light, the
nuptial union becomes the most sacred and revered of all our human acts
because it completes us perfectly for we live the gift of love. St. John Paul in
his Apostolic Letter defines and describes the great mystery of the feminine
and masculine

> We read that man cannot exist "alone" (cf. Gen 2:18); he can exist
> only as a "unity of the two", and therefore in relation to another hu-
> man person. It is a question here of a mutual relationship: man to
> woman and woman to man. Being a person in the image and like-
> ness of God thus also involves existing in a relationship, in relation
> to the other "I". This is a prelude to the definitive self-revelation of
> the Triune God: a living unity in the communion of the Father,
> Son and Holy Spirit.[4]

3. Teresa of Avila, *Life of St. Teresa*, 22.21.
4. John Paul II, *Mulieris Dignitatem*, sec. 7.

St. John Paul II, the poet and mystic, creates *The Theology of the Body* revealing intimacy in the context of the covenant: a mutual gift exchange. This describes the transformative power of love which allegorically reveals the power of the Holy Spirit uniting us mystically to the Divine Bridegroom.

We, who embark on theosis, now read the scriptures in light of this nuptial theme and sense the beauty contained in the narratives as our invitation to enter intimately into the interior life of the Trinity. In our meditation, especially on the acts of creation, we hear the echo of God's original purpose of creation: a marital union with God. Yet, St. John Paul II, as does the Song of Songs, reminds us to restrain our desires to unite ourselves to the Bridegroom and go cautiously. This revelation has meanings and mysteries so deep and hidden from our direct vision, God must prepare our hearts slowly otherwise we may rush too quickly and never truly understand and encounter the great epiphanies that will come from our *Lectio Divina*.

These epiphanies cannot be earned or bought as some try to do; they are the Secret Ladder in Jacob's Dream a theophany, a pure gift of the Father's love coming down from heaven to fill our hearts because we dared to enter the holy dialogue.

We are living this mystery, re-creation, and yet, we do not fully understand it, nor will we ever penetrate the depths and breath of the created universe, much less will we ever comprehend the Divine Trinity. Artists and mystics, however, through their *Lectio Divina* expose these divine mysteries and through prayer enter a dialogue which speaks to heart to heart, face to face unveiling the beauty of love, just as a bride unveils herself on her wedding night.

No one could see God, not even Moses; we, however, more privileged than Moses, see the beauty of the Father when we read, meditate, pray, and finally contemplate the Word, for this Word is made flesh and dwells not merely with us but within us through the Spirit because he states, "Whoever has seen me has seen the Father. How can you say, 'Show us the Father'? Do you not believe that I am in the Father and the Father is in me?" (John 14:9–10). *Lectio Divina* is a dialogue with the Divine Artisan who is the Great I AM seeking a conversation with us as he did with Jacob. He comes to us down the ladder appearing to us as I AM and we are to see ourselves as His. In this relationship, we see our personal divine dignity: I am a thou to the Great I AM encountering the Face of the Father through the Words of the Son. This is my identity. I am a thou: a person of greatest value to the Father who wants me to be one with him, as Jesus states directly.

> The glory that you have given me I have given to them, that they may be one even as we are one, I in them and you in me, that they may become perfectly one, so that the world may know that you sent me and loved them even as you loved me. (John 17:22–23)

Jesus introduces this new reality, oneness with the Divine revealing the Kingdom of Heaven is a Wedding Banquet. Not the one in the Garden of Eden, which was lost and divorced in the Fall, but the Wedding Banquet, the Lamb's High Feast in heaven. St. John witnesses to this allegory,

> I saw the holy city, new Jerusalem, coming down out of heaven from God, prepared as a bride adorned for her husband. And I heard a loud voice from the throne saying, "Behold, the dwelling place of God is with man. He will dwell with them, and they will be his people, and God himself will be with them as their God." (Rev 21:2–3)

Revelation shows us who we are: the new Holy Jerusalem, the body and bride of Christ.

> Come here, I will show you the bride, the Lamb's wife. And he carried me away in the spirit to a great and high mountain, and showed me that great city, the holy Jerusalem, descending out of heaven from God. (Rev 21:9)

Jesus is the Bridegroom who leaves his Heavenly Father, descends down the ladder to commune with us. He is the Light who clothed Adam and Eve, now re-creating and showing us who God is, Our Father. In this light, we too can commune as Adam and Eve communed with the Father intimately hand in hand. This image of Jerusalem descending from heaven is his Body, the Church and each individual in his Church becomes his bride. We become one with him, as does husband and wife become one in body, mind, heart, and soul.

COVENANTAL UNDERSTANDING

Recognizing Jesus as our Bridegroom, he invites us into his life. This invitation is our greatest treasure, we his pearl, see him as our sole Pearl. This singular relationship that Jesus has with his Church, and we are his Church, his bride, reveals the purpose and center of our human life: Oneness with the Divine found in theosis.

As St. Augustine says, God promises us so much and gives us riches beyond pearls, he gives us the riches of the Kingdom as we contemplate the heavenly Jerusalem.

We, the bride, discover this mystical and divine union only when our faith has matured. The mystic then experiences both in body and soul the encounter with the Truth, Beauty, and Goodness of God. He shares himself with us, imparting more than just a written revelation; it is the *Communio Personarum*, the indwelling of the same Spirit that hovered over the waters. This same Spirit, that breathed life into the clay, now hovers over us as the New Pentecost. This indwelling, then, constantly creates us, uniting us into a covenantal bond in which the Holy Spirit dwells mysteriously and personally within each human heart. We call it a covenant: an exchange of persons because God exchanges himself totally and fruitfully inviting us to give our self to him faithfully and freely. In this exchange, we create a sacred, family bond that cannot be broken: a mystical marriage.

Only through covenantal relationships do we understand Sacred Scriptures for we read scripture under a different rubric. It is not literal, but typological in which signs and symbols unveil the hidden meanings that the literal sense contains. Our reading of scripture this way leads to mystical contemplation encountering the Face of the Father, allowing God to infuse his divine truth, goodness, and beauty in us.

> I saw no temple in the city, for its temple is the Lord God the Almighty and the Lamb. And the city has no need of sun or moon to shine on it, for the glory of God gives it light, and its lamp is the Lamb. (Rev 21:2)

St. John Paul II developed an extraordinarily consistent theology based in the spiritual gifts of *Lectio Divina* which is the source of the New Evangelization and theosis, the source of the coming of the New Pentecost. Out of passion, God created us. His Pathos rescued us from the powers of evil and transfigured us, removing our exile which divorced us from the Beatific Vision. Building on these understandings, St. John Paul II developed programs of the New Evangelization and New Pentecost to guide the living stream of the Catholic Church. His cry "Do not be afraid!" still rings in our hearts, for we recognize that he was without fear because he had seen God's action in his life, world, and beloved Catholic Church.

St. John Paul II's call for a New Evangelization and Pentecost still lingers as a prophecy: Accompany Jesus Christ and tell others of the way of Christian perfection, of theosis, that brings us to the power of the new Jerusalem, of living holiness, the Trinity dwelling within our minds, hearts, and souls.

BIBLIOGRAPHY

Augustine. *Commentary on Psalms*. Edited by E. Dekkers and J. Fraipont. CCSL 40. Turnhout: Brepols, 1990.

———. *Confessions*. Translated by John K. Ryan. Garden City, NY: Image, 1960.

———. *Let Us Sing to the Lord a Song of Love*. https://www.vatican.va/spirit/documents/spirit_20010508_agostino-vescovo_en.html.

———. *De Musica*. In *Philosophies of Art and Beauty*, edited by Albert Hofstadter and Richard Kuhns, 185–202. Chicago: University of Chicago Press, 1976.

———. *The Trinity*. Translated by Edmund Hill. Hyde Park, NY: New City, 1991.

Aumann, Jordan. *Spiritual Theology*. New York: Continuum, 2006.

Aquinas, Thomas. *Summa Theologiae*. https://www.newadvent.org/summa/.

Barron, Robert. *Word on Fire Vatican II Collection*. Park Ridge, IL: Word on Fire, 2021.

Béchard, Dean P., ed. *The Scripture Documents: An Anthology of Official Catholic Teachings*. Collegeville, MN: Liturgical, 2001.

Benedict XII, Pope. *Benedictus Deus: On the Beatific Vision of God*. https://www.papalencyclicals.net/ben12/b12bdeus.htm.

Benedict XVI, Pope. *Mass, Imposition of the Pallium and Conferral of the Fisherman's Ring for the Beginning of the Petrine Ministry of the Bishop of Rome*. https://www.vatican.va/content/benedict-xvi/en/homilies/2005/documents/hf_ben-xvi_hom_20050424_inizio-pontificato.html.

———. "Meeting with Artists." http://www.vatican.va/content/benedict-xvi/en/speeches/2009/november/documents/hf_ben-xvi_spe_20091121_artisti.html.

———. "Participants in a Meeting Organized by the Catholic Fraternity of Charismatic Covenant Communities and Fellowships." https://www.vatican.va/content/benedict-xvi/en/speeches/2008/october/documents/hf_ben-xvi_spe_20081031_carismatici.html.

———. "Renewal in the Holy Spirit." http://www.vatican.va/content/benedict-xvi/en/speeches/2012/may/documents/hf_ben-xvi_spe_20120526_rinnov-spirito.html.

———. *The Via Pulchritudinis, Privileged Pathway for Evangelization and Dialogue*. https://www.vatican.va/roman_curia/pontifical_councils/cultr/documents/rc_pc_cultr_doc_20060327_plenary-assembly_final-document_en.html.

Bernard of Clairvaux. *Treatises II: Steps of Humility and Pride and On Loving God*. Kalamazoo, MI: Cistercian, 1980.

Boczek, Macon. "Faith as an "Essential Likeness" of Human and Divine Reason: Karol Wojtyla's Dissertation on Faith in the Mystical Writings of Saint John of the Cross." PhD diss., Kent State University, 2012.

Catherine of Siena. *The Dialogue*. Translated by Suzanne Noffke. New York: Paulist, 1980.

Caussade, Jean Pierre de. *Abandonment to Divine Providence*. New York: Image, 1975.

Catechism of the Catholic Church. https://www.vatican.va/archive/ENG0015/_INDEX. HTM.

Clendenin, Daniel B. "Partakers of Divinity: The Orthodox Doctrine of Theosis." *Journal of the Evangelical Theological Society* 37.3 (1994) 369–75.

Denzinger, Henry. *The Sources of Catholic Dogma*. Edited by Peter Hunermann. San Francisco: Ignatius, 2012.

Didymus of Alexandria. *Treatise on the Trinity*. In vol. 2 of "Divine Office: The Liturgy of the Hours." New York: Catholic Book, 1975.

EWTN. "Our Lady of Fatima." https://www.ewtn.com/catholicism/saints/our-lady-of-fatima-423.

Fehlner, F. I. *St. Maximilian Ma. Kolbe, Martyr of Charity, Pneumatologist: His Theology of the Holy Spirit*. New Bedford, MA: Academy of the Immaculate, 2004.

Francis, Pope. "Greetings of His Holiness Pope France to the Artists of the Christmas Concert in the Vatican." https://www.vatican.va/content/francesco/en/speeches/2020/december/documents/papa-francesco_20201212_artisti-concertodinatale.html.

Francis of Assisi. "*Sancta Maria Virgo*." http://www.ibreviary.com/m2/preghiere.php?tipo=Preghiera&id=211#holyvm.

Fénelon, Francois de Salignac de La Mothe. *The Archbishop of Cambray's Dissertation on Pure Love, with an Account of the Life and Writings of the Lady, for Whose Sake the Archbishop was Banished from Court*. London: Thomson, 1750.

———. *The Maxims of the Saints Explained, concerning the Interior Life*. Bordeaux, 1913.

Ghosn, Margaret. *The Maronite Divine Liturgy of St. James*. https://www.olol.org.au/the-maronite-tradition/the-maronite-divine-liturgy.

Guigo II the Carthusian. *The Ladder of Monks*. Translated by Sr. Pascale-Cominique Nau. Lulu.com, 2012.

Guyon, Jeanne de la Mothe. *Autobiography of Madame Guyon*. Translated by Thomas Taylor Allen. 2 vols. London: Paul, Trench, Trubner, 1897.

———. *Divine Love: The Emblems of Madame Jeanne Guyon and Otto van Veen*. Translated by Nancy Carol James. Eugene, OR: Pickwick, 2019.

———. *Jeanne Guyon's Apocalyptic Universe: Her Biblical Commentary on Revelation with Reflections on the Interior Life*. Translated by Nancy Carol James. Eugene, OR: Pickwick, 2019.

———. *Jeanne Guyon's Christian Worldview: Her Biblical Commentaries on Galatians, Ephesians, and Colossians with Explanations and Reflections on the Interior Life*. Translated by Nancy Carol James. Eugene, OR: Pickwick, 2018.

———. *Jeanne Guyon's Interior Faith: Her Biblical Commentary on the Gospel of Luke with Reflections on the Interior Life*. Translated by Nancy Carol James. Eugene, OR: Pickwick, 2019.

———. *Jeanne Guyon's Mystical Perfection through Eucharistic Suffering*. Translated by Nancy Carol James. Eugene, OR: Pickwick, 2020.

———. *The Soul, Lover of God*. Translated by Nancy Carol James. New York: University Press of America, 2014.

———. *The Way of the Child Jesus: Our Model of Perfection*. Translated by Nancy Carol James. Arlington, VA: European Emblems, 2015.

Irenaeus. *Against Heresies*. https://www.newadvent.org/fathers/0103.htm.

James, Nancy C. "The Apophatic Mysticism of Madame Guyon." PhD diss., University of Virginia, 1998.

———. *The Complete Madame Guyon.* Brewster, MA: Paraclete, 2011.

———. *I, Jeanne Guyon.* Jacksonville, FL: Seedsowers, 2014.

———. *The Pure Love of Madame Guyon.* New York: University Press of America, 2007.

James, Nancy C., and Sharon D. Voros. *Bastille Witness: The Prison Autobiography of Madame Guyon.* New York: University Press of America, 2012.

James, William. *Varieties of Religious Experience.* New York: Collier, 1961.

John XXIII, Pope. "Opening Address to the Council." https://www.vatican.va/content/john-xxiii/la/apost_constitutions/1961/documents/hf_j-xxiii_apc_19611225_humanae-salutis.html.

John of the Cross. *The Ascent of Mount Carmel.* In *The Collected Works of St. John of the Cross,* translated by Kieran Kavanaugh and Orilio Rodriguez, 101–352. 3rd ed. Washington DC: ICS, 2017.

———. *Dark Night of the Soul.* Translated by E. Allison Peers. Garden City, NY: Image, 1959.

———. *The Spiritual Canticle.* In *The Collected Works of St. John of the Cross,* translated by Kieran Kavanaugh and Orilio Rodriguez, 461–632. 3rd ed. Washington DC: ICS, 2017.

———. *The Poems of Saint John of the Cross.* Translated by Willis Barnstone. Bloomington: Indiana University Press, 1968.

John Paul II, Pope. *By the Communion of Persons Man Becomes the Image of God.* https://www.vatican.va/content/john-paul-ii/en/audiences/1979/documents/hf_jp-ii_aud_19791114.html.

———. *Centimus Annus.* https://www.vatican.va/content/john-paul-ii/en/encyclicals/documents/hf_jp-ii_enc_01051991_centesimus-annus.html.

———. *Dominum et Vivificantum.* https://www.vatican.va/content/john-paul-ii/en/encyclicals/documents/hf_jp-ii_enc_18051986_dominum-et-vivificantem.html.

———. *Ecclesia de Eucharistia.* https://www.vatican.va/holy_father/special_features/encyclicals/documents/hf_jp-ii_enc_20030417_ecclesia_eucharistia_en.html.

———. *Evangelium Vitae.* https://www.vatican.va/content/john-paul-ii/en/encyclicals/documents/hf_jp-ii_enc_25031995_evangelium-vitae.html.

———. *Faith according to Saint John of the Cross.* Translated by Jordan Aumann. San Francisco: Ignatius, 1981.

———. "General Audience, April 5, 2000." https://www.vatican.va/content/john-paul-ii/en/audiences/2000/documents/hf_jp-ii_aud_20000405.html.

———. "General Audience, August 18, 1999." https://www.vatican.va/content/john-paul-ii/en/audiences/1999/documents/hf_jp-ii_aud_18081999.html.

———. "General Audience, March 12, 1986." https://www.vatican.va/content/john-paul-ii/it/audiences/1986/documents/hf_jp-ii_aud_19860312.html.

———. "General Audience, May 28, 1997." https://www.vatican.va/content/john-paul-ii/en/audiences/1997/documents/hf_jp-ii_aud_28051997.html.

———. "General Audience, October 1, 1986." https://www.vatican.va/content/john-paul-ii/it/audiences/1986/documents/hf_jp-ii_aud_19861001.html.

———. "General Audience, October 8, 1986." https://www.vatican.va/content/john-paul-ii/it/audiences/1986/documents/hf_jp-ii_aud_19861008.html.

———. "General Audience, October 29, 1986." https://www.vatican.va/content/john-paul-ii/it/audiences/1986/documents/hf_jp-ii_aud_19861029.html.

———. "General Audience, November 19, 2003." https://www.vatican.va/content/john-paul-ii/en/audiences/2003/documents/hf_jp-ii_aud_20031119.html.

———. *Jesus Sent by the Father for the Salvation of the World*. http://www.vatican.va/jubilee_2000/magazine/documents/ju_mag_01041998_p-24_en.html.

———. *Letter to Artists*. https://www.vatican.va/content/john-paul-ii/en/letters/1999/documents/hf_jp-ii_let_23041999_artists.html.

———. *Mass of Pentecost*. https://www.vatican.va/content/john-paul-ii/en/homilies/2001/documents/hf_jp-ii_hom_20010603_pentecoste.html.

———. *Mulieris Dignitatem*. https://www.vatican.va/content/john-paul-ii/en/apost_letters/1988/documents/hf_jp-ii_apl_19880815_mulieris-dignitatem.html.

———. *Novo Millennio Ineunte*. http://www.vatican.va/content/john-paulii/en/apost_letters/2001/documents/hf_jp-ii_apl_20010106_novo-millennio-ineunte.html.

———. *Private Audience of Pope John Paul II with ICCRS Council*. In *Contemporary Peoples of the Spirit*, edited by Stanley M. Burgress, 279. New York: New York University Press, 2011.

———. *Reconciliation and Penance*. https://www.vatican.va/content/john-paul-ii/en/apost_exhortations/documents/hf_jp-ii_exh_02121984_reconciliatio-et-paenitentia.html.

———. *The Redemption of the Body and Sacramentality of Marriage (Theology of the Body)*. https://d2y1pz2y630308.cloudfront.net/2232/documents/2016/9/theology_of_the_body.pdf.

———. *Redemptoris Mater*. https://www.vatican.va/content/john-paul-ii/en/encyclicals/documents/hf_jp-ii_enc_25031987_redemptoris-mater.html.

———. *Redemptor Hominis*. https://www.vatican.va/content/john-paul-ii/en/encyclicals/documents/hf_jp-ii_enc_04031979_redemptor-hominis.html.

———. *Salvifici Doloris*. https://www.vatican.va/content/john-paul-ii/en/apost_letters/1984/documents/hf_jp-ii_apl_11021984_salvifici-doloris.html.

———. "Speech to Ecclesial Movements and New Communities." https://www.vatican.va/content/john-paul-ii/en/speeches/1998/may/documents/hf_jp-ii_spe_19980530_riflessioni.html.

———. *Solemnity of Pentecost*. https://www.vatican.va/content/john-paul-ii/en/homilies/1998/documents/hf_jp-ii_hom_31051998.html.

———. "To the Conference Studying the Implementation of the Second Vatican Council." https://www.vatican.va/content/john-paul-ii/en/speeches/2000/jan-mar/documents/hf_jp-ii_spe_20000227_vatican-council-ii.html.

———. "To Leaders of Renewal in the Spirit." https://www.vatican.va/content/john-paul-ii/en/speeches/1998/april/documents/hf_jp-ii_spe_19980404_spirito-santo.html.

———. *Veritatis Splendor*. https://www.vatican.va/content/john-paul-ii/en/encyclicals/documents/hf_jp-ii_enc_06081993_veritatis-splendor.html.

Kolbe, Maximilian Maria. *Scritti di Massimiliano Kolbe*. Rome, 1997.

Komonchak, Joseph A. "Pope John XXIII and the Idea of an Ecumenical Council." https://jakomonchak.files.wordpress.com/2012/01/john-xxiii-idea-of-a-council.pdf.

Kuffel, Thomas P. "St. Thomas' Method of Biblical Exegesis." *Roman Theological Forum* 38 (1991). http://www.rtforum.org/lt/lt38.html.

Mattei, Roberto de. "Reflections on the Liturgical Reform." In *Looking Again at the Question of the Liturgy with Cardinal Ratzinger*, edited by Alcuin Reid, 141. Farnborough: Saint Michael's Abbey, 2003.

Maximus the Confessor. *Various Texts on Theology, the Divine Economy, and Virtue and Vice.* https://orthodoxchurchfathers.com/fathers/philokalia/maximus-the-confessor-various-texts-on-theology-the-divine-economy-and-virtue-an.html.

Nicodemus the Hagiorite. *Nicodemus of the Holy Mountain: A Handbook of Spiritual Counsel.* Translated by Peter A. Chamberas. New York: Paulist, 1989.

Paul VI, Pope. *Apostolic Constitution Paenitemini.* http://www.vatican.va/content/paul-vi/en/apost_constitutions/documents/hf_p-vi_apc_19660217_paenitemini.html.

———. *Dei Verbum.* https://www.vatican.va/archive/hist_councils/ii_vatican_council/documents/vat-ii_const_19651118_dei-verbum_en.html.

———. *Gaudete in Domino.* https://www.vatican.va/content/paul-vi/en/apost_exhortations/documents/hf_p-vi_exh_19750509_gaudete-in-domino.html.

———. *The Holy Spirit Animator and Sanctifier of the Church.* https://www.vatican.va/content/paul-vi/it/audiences/1972/documents/hf_p-vi_aud_19721129.html.

———. *Lumen Gentium.* https://www.vatican.va/archive/hist_councils/ii_vatican_council/documents/vat-ii_const_19641121_lumen-gentium_en.html.

———. *"Veni, Creator Spiritus . . . Consolator optime . . . Dulcis Hospes animae."* https://www.vatican.va/content/paul-vi/it/audiences/1973/documents/hf_p-vi_aud_19730523.html.

Percy, Walker. *Love in the Ruins.* New York: Farrar, Straus, and Giroux, 1971.

———. *The Thanatos Syndrome.* New York: Farrar, Straus, and Giroux, 1987.

Pius IX, Pope. *Ineffabilis Deus: The Immaculate Conception.* https://www.papalencyclicals.net/pius09/p9ineff.htm.

———. *Quanto conficiamur moerore.* https://www.papalencyclicals.net/pius09/p9quanto.htm.

Pocetto, Alexander T. "The Image of Jacob's Ladder in the Writings of St. Francis de Sales." http://hosted.desales.edu/files/salesian/PDF/PocettoJacobsLadder.pdf.

Ricoeur, Paul. *Fallible Man.* Translated by Charles A Kelbley. New York: Fordham University Press, 1986.

———. *The Rule of Metaphor.* Translated by Robert Czerny. Toronto: University of Toronto Press, 1981.

———. *The Symbolism of Evil.* Translated by Emerson Buchanan. New York: Harper & Row, 1969.

Schönborn, Christoph Cardinal. "On Love and Friendship." https://www.thomasaquinas.edu/news/cardinal-schonborn-love-and-friendship.

Second Vatican Council. *The Word on Fire Vatican II Collection.* Park Ridge, IL: Word on Fire, 2021.

Teresa of Avila. *Life of St. Teresa.* Translated by David Lewis. 3rd ed. New York: Benzinger Bros., 1904.

Underhill, Evelyn. *Mysticism: A Study in the Nature and Development of Man's Spiritual Consciousness.* 12th ed. Cleveland: World, 1965.

Weigel, George. *Witness to Hope.* New York: HarperCollins, 1999.

SUBJECT INDEX